A B O V E · T H E · F A L L S

Left to right: Grant McConachie, George Dalziel and Frank Burton beside Dalziel's newly purchased Curtiss Robin.

A B O V E · T H E · F A L L S

JOHN HARRIS

VICTORIA · VANCOUVER · CALGARY

TouchWood Editions	TouchWood Editions
#108–17665 66A Avenue	PO Box 468
Surrey, BC V3S 2A7	Custer, WA
www.touchwoodeditions.com	98240-0468

LIBRARY AND ARCHIVES CANADA CATALOGUING IN PUBLICATION
Harris, John, 1942–
     Above the falls / John Harris.

ISBN 978-1-894898-55-3

     1. Dalziel, George, ?–1982—Fiction. 2. Trapping—Northwest
Territories—South Nahanni River Valley—History—Fiction. 3. South
Nahanni River Valley (N.W.T.)—History—Fiction. I. Title.

PS8615.A769A62 2007   C813'.6   C2007-901144-6

LIBRARY OF CONGRESS CONTROL NUMBER: 2006907469

Edited by Marlyn Horsdal
Proofread by Vivian Sinclair
Book design by Jacqui Thomas
Cover image of Brintnell Creek by Vivien Lougheed
Frontispiece photo supplied by B. Richardson, courtesy of Aviation Museum of Alberta
Printed and bound in Canada by Friesens

TouchWood Editions acknowledges the financial support for its publishing program
from the Government of Canada through the Book Publishing Industry Development
Program (BPIDP), Canada Council for the Arts, and the province of British Columbia
through the British Columbia Arts Council and the Book Publishing Tax Credit.

BRITISH COLUMBIA
ARTS COUNCIL
Supported by the Province of British Columbia

The Canada Council | Le Conseil des Arts
for the Arts | du Canada

*This book has been produced on 100% post-consumer recycled paper, processed chlorine free and
printed with vegetable-based dyes.*

To A.C. Lewis, author of *Nahanni Remembered*

ACKNOWLEDGMENTS

My wife, Vivien Lougheed, and editor Marlyn Horsdal got me going on the story and kept me at it. Al Lewis, Dick North and Raymond Patterson, Nahanni pioneers, wrote books describing the characters and their lives. Lewis told me other parts of his story and described Harry Vandaele in more detail than he'd given in his book. Moira Farrow wrote a valuable description of Albert Faille. Howell Martyn, in 1952, walked some of the route taken by Wade and Eppler in the book. He described it to me and gave me Norm Thomas's photos and unpublished description of the country.

W. D. Addison & Associates, working for Parks Canada, interviewed the Nahanni pioneers in the last years of their lives. Sherry Bradford gave me access to her father George Dalziel's notebooks and photos, and described him to me. Her brother, Byron Dalziel, provided more information. David Raup sent me his father Hugh Miller Raup's photos and book about Glacier Lake. Dudley Bolyard sent me his geological description of the lake and the Cirque of the Unclimbables.

Bob Brown, my brother-in-law, and Sheldon Clare helped me with the guns and, along with Audrey McClellan, Bruce Serafin and my daughter, Jennifer Harris, did story edits at the early stages of the book. The College of New Caledonia, from which I recently retired, continues to provide me with working space, research assistance and encouragement.

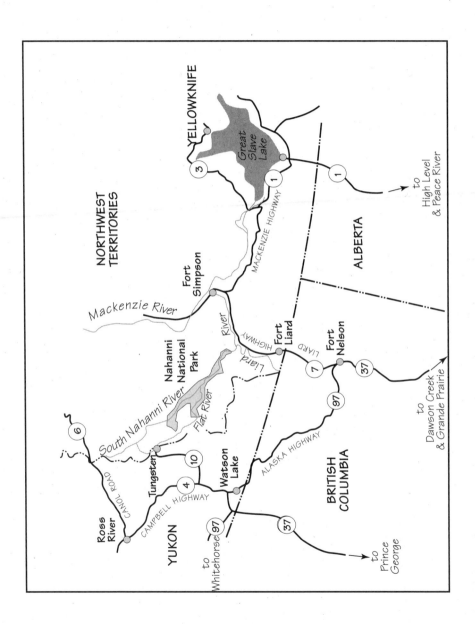

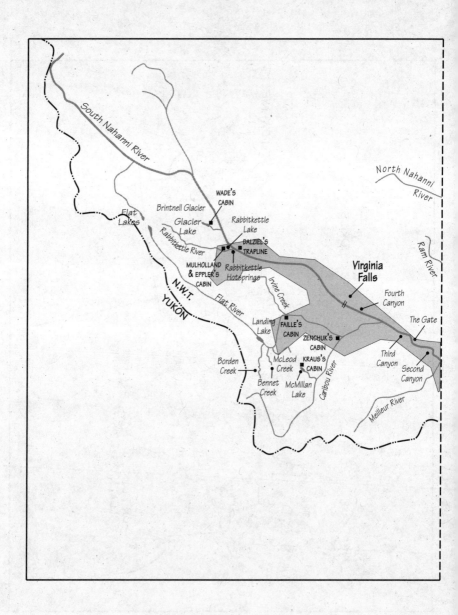

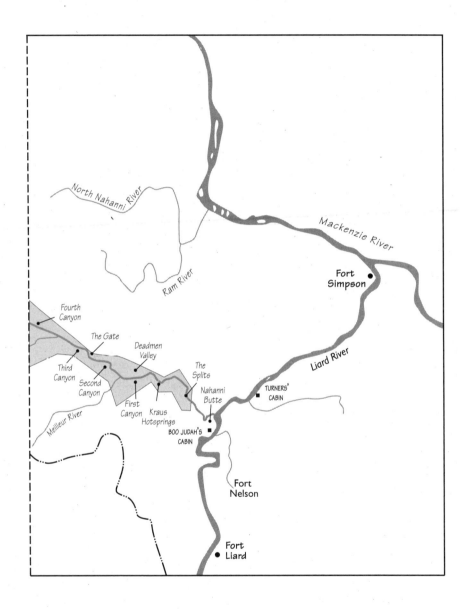

North Nahanni River

Mackenzie River

Ram River

Fort Simpson

Fourth Canyon

The Gate

Deadmen Valley

Third Canyon

Second Canyon

The Splits

First Canyon

Kraus Hotsprings

Nahanni Butte

Liard River

TURNERS' CABIN

Meilleur River

BOO JUDAH'S CABIN

Fort Nelson

Fort Liard

Above the falls? In the 1930s, the only whites who knew anything about that area were Faille, Dalziel and maybe Zenchuk.

—AL LEWIS

1

NOT FAR OUT on a frozen lake, a tall, slim man was chopping at a water hole with an axe, his breath rising in a steady stream and hovering in a cloud above his head. He wore a toque, a heavy, red-and-black plaid wool shirt, wool pants held up by red suspenders, moccasins and long sheep-skin mitts. He was remembering to be careful, to do things slowly, to hang on tight so that if the handle hit the rim of the hole, the axe wouldn't jerk out of his hands and disappear into the lake. He checked the axe head regularly, making sure it was tight.

"We only got two of these, Joe," Bill had said. "And the spare one ain't so good."

A Newfoundland dog was standing on the ice nearby, watching, tail wagging slowly.

Behind Joe and his dog was a sod-roofed log cabin, hud-dled in snow. Smoke billowed from the chimney and disap-peared immediately into the grey, low-hanging clouds. The cabin's gabled end, with a tiny window, faced the lake. Joe's snowshoes were propped against the wall, and a 45-gallon fuel drum with the letters DAL painted on its side sat near the trail leading from the cabin to the lake. Light, barely perceptible snowflakes were falling onto the lake and the spruce-furred hills around it.

Joe rested a moment, gazing toward the far end of the lake. Soon, Bill would appear there and cross the lake to the cabin. They would compare each other's catches from their respective parts of the trapline.

A couple of hours earlier, Joe had come in with three marten, a fox and a wolverine, the last rare according to the boys in Fort Simpson, worth little at the trading post but saleable locally at a good price as parka trim. All of Joe's catch was now hanging from the cabin ceiling, defrosting. Tomorrow, he would start pelting and scraping.

The wolverine had had his paw well in the set and hadn't been there for long, still jerking hard on the chain and gnawing on it and his own leg, scarcely even looking up when Joe appeared. A shot to the head finished it. It was the first time he'd ever had to shoot something on the line, shells being expensive, as Bill had also pointed out. But there was no way he was going to try clubbing the thing to death.

Wolverine hardly ever got caught in traps. Maybe Bill would have some stories and theories about this one. It didn't look emaciated from sickness, old age or hunger; its coat glistened like silk. It might have been young and inexperienced. Some of the locals believed that the animal was subject to snow blindness. If so, it could have walked into the trap.

Joe's recent catch, if he prepared the pelts right, was

worth maybe $60 down at the post, more money than he'd ever earned before over only three days. Five days altogether, if you counted preparation. And so far, after only three months, they had, Bill figured, over $1,000 worth of marten and lynx in the cache. Bill was obviously happy. It had taken a month, down along the Liard River, to bring in $100. They'd put in almost three months there when the pilot suggested flying to the lake. "It's the best marten country I know of," he'd said. "And there's no one working it. I'm letting my camp below the hotsprings sit idle until next year. You guys will have the place to yourselves."

And the flight in cost only $100.

When Bill came across the lake with his catch, they'd cook some moose steak. Then, an evening at cards, trying to beat the unbeatable Bill Eppler. The prize, Bill had announced on their first night in camp, was the one bed in the cabin, a pole-box on four blocks of firewood. The box held spruce boughs—the bed's mattress. There was a question of whether it was any more comfortable than the pile of boughs kept beneath it for spreading a second bed on the floor, but Bill always said that it was a "spiritual" thing, that the person in the official bed slept "on a higher plane."

So far, Joe had spent only a couple of nights on the real bed.

"Bill's one of the best," Joe's older brother, Jack, had said. "You'll learn right from him, and he's an easy man to be with."

The young man resumed chopping, then took his bucket, got down on his knees and pushed it into the hole. To reach water, he had to get his head and shoulders below the surface of the ice. He rose again, slowly, the bucket full, then stood for a moment, his gaze at the far end of the lake. A breeze had come up; it was blowing into his face from the south.

"Gettin' warmer," he said. "Gonna blizzard, maybe, Ghengis." The dog's tail wagged faster. "Bill should be close."

He picked up the axe with his free hand and walked the path to the cabin. When he reached the door he leaned the axe against the frame and reached for the door handle, only to be startled by a loud growl and then a rush of frantic barking from Ghengis. As he turned to look, a gunshot exploded. Ghengis tumbled onto the snow a few yards away and lay still.

A man stood at the edge of the clearing, his rifle not shouldered but held at hip level, still pointed at Ghengis. He was tall, heavy and bearded, and clad in fur—a hat with ear flaps, a thick coat and leggings. His pack was topped with a bulky sleeping bag.

Joe scarcely looked at him. He was staring in disbelief at Ghengis. "What the bloody hell did you do that for?"

"Your dog was coming at me."

"I guess so! I woulda called him off. Where'd you come from?"

"How long you been here?"

"Three months."

"That your line back there?"

The young man looked up and saw that his questioner's rifle was now pointing at him, and this made him angry. "Who are you?"

"You with a partner?"

"I said who are you?"

"Maybe you already know who I am. Maybe you been watching me."

"Just tell me your name, if you can remember it."

A shot rang out, and Joe spun around and slumped silently into the snow, the water bucket tipping as he went down.

The man with the rifle walked toward the cabin and stood for a while examining the patch of blood spreading brightly through the young man's shirt. Then he said, "Francis John Wade, Private, K-2558."

He turned, walked to the shore of the lake and stood scanning the shoreline carefully. Then he focused his attention on the fuel drum. "The pilot," he said. He returned to the cabin and removed his pack and showshoes, propping them against the wall. Pushing the cabin door open, he disappeared inside, emerging a few minutes later with a tin of tobacco. He opened the tin, looked inside, pulled a lighter out of it, examined the lighter, turning it around in his hands, then dropped it back in the tin and stuck the tin under his arm. Seizing his snowshoes, he carried them into the trees behind the cabin.

The cache was uncovered, a ladder against its front and a white tarp hanging down from its back. A long wooden toboggan leaned against one of the support trees, a small tarp tucked into its tie-down rope. Wade mounted the ladder and examined the contents of the cache. He picked up a rifle and examined it.

"Thirty-thirty," he said. He reached back into the cache

and produced a box of shells. He descended the ladder, propped the rifle against a tree, placed the shells on the snow and ascended again.

"Can of paint. Roll of canvas. Must've been planning some improvements. Some food. I can use that. A bit of moose meat."

He reached farther into the cache. "Good take of marten," he mumbled. Two bundles of pelts hit the ground.

"Lynx." Another bundle hit the ground.

Wade came back down the ladder carrying a couple of small food bags, which he loaded into his pack. He laid the toboggan on the snow and piled the bundled pelts onto it, putting the rifle and box of shells in the middle of the pile. It was snowing more heavily, so he tied the whole load down with the small tarp and a rope that was already attached to the toboggan's side.

Back at the cabin, he rolled his victim over and seized him under the shoulders, dragging him and the water bucket, now frozen in the dead man's hand, inside. He took the dog by a hind leg and dragged him into the cabin too. Then, moving faster, he walked toward the lake. He kicked the fuel barrel loose from the frozen ground, pushed it over and rolled it to the cabin door, where he stood it up. He used the axe to tap the spigot open and then threw the axe into the cabin and pushed the barrel after it.

He ran for the cache. There was silence for two, three minutes, and then a stunning blast kicked out the upper logs of the cabin walls and lifted the roof. The door and its frame cartwheeled across the clearing. The roof fell back into the cabin as a tower of flame shot up and out, igniting needles and branches on the surrounding trees.

A few minutes later, Wade stepped into the clearing. He was making a cigarette. He finished it, watching the flames rolling up from the cabin in giant waves, feeling the blistering heat on his face. He picked up a burning branch that had fallen beside him and lit the cigarette. Smiling, he congratulated himself on having noticed the fuel barrel. All he'd had to do was stoke up the fire and leave the stove door open.

The barrel had been near full. There'd be nothing left by the time the fire burned down.

Back at the cache, he strapped on his snowshoes, shouldered his pack, picked up the rope of the toboggan and headed north.

2

THREE MILES WEST of the cabin, there was a stand of old spruce trees along the banks of the Rabbitkettle River, which ran past the south end of the lake into a much bigger river, the South Nahanni. The Rabbitkettle took the lake's overflow through a marsh that had stunted tamarack trees in bunched stands around its perimeter, and open areas bordered by willow in its centre. Where the spruce ended and the tamaracks started, Bill Eppler was standing at attention, listening.

He was a short, trim man with a pug nose, thin lips and the ruddy skin of a man who has spent his life outside. His eyes were hidden behind a pair of wire-framed sunglasses. A freshly rolled cigarette, unlit, stuck out of the side of his mouth. He wore a beret, fur coat, wool leggings and snowshoes, and had a pack on his back with a sleeping bag strapped on top. A toboggan was just behind him, with a rifle laid carefully along the top of three corpses—two marten and a fox. Immediately behind the toboggan a Newfoundland dog, with saddlebags, waited. The handle of a hatchet stuck out of one of the bags.

The dog began to whine.

"Shh, Kubla," said Eppler. "What was that?"

Through the light but accelerating snowfall, he saw in the distance a cloud of black smoke.

"What in hell!" Eppler yanked the cigarette out of his mouth and stuffed it in his pocket. He reached around with his other hand, grabbed the rifle and began to run, his snowshoes hardly lifting, sliding smoothly along the barely visible path that led back to the cabin. Kubla hurried around the toboggan and followed.

Partway through the marsh, Eppler stopped to catch his breath. The smoke was now a column, rising above the trees and then floating north.

When he burst through the scrub spruce at the edge of the lake, he saw the cabin aflame, a bright orange light raging against the universal grayness of sky, lake and forest. He rushed across the ice. As he approached the cabin, the fire was so hot that he could scarcely get closer than the shore. Entire trees were burning along the edge of the clearing. He circled behind the cabin, trying to see into the flames, but Kubla drew his attention by lunging toward the cache. Eppler immediately squatted down beside a tree, lifting his rifle sideways and levering a cartridge into the chamber. He watched the dog, who was now moving back and forth by the cache, nose near the ground and hackles up. Eppler examined the woods carefully, then moved toward Kubla.

The tracks of someone in large snowshoes, pulling a loaded toboggan, led north, in the direction of Joe's part of the trapline. Some of the snowshoe webbing had been repaired.

"It ain't Joe, is it, boy?" he muttered.

He followed the tracks.

"He's goin' back the way he came. No dog."

In an open area about 15 minutes from the cabin, Kubla stopped near a tree by the side of the trail, sniffing. Eppler examined the ground near Kubla's nose, then scooped up a handful of freshly fallen snow and filtered it through his fingers. A cigarette butt.

"Joe don't smoke."

He pushed on quickly, but after an hour he was just following the trapline, with Kubla behind, finding no scent to follow; the blizzard, at full force now, had erased the track. At the end of the line he circled out through the bush, looking for broken branches or tracks protected by sheltering bushes, but it was too dark.

He stopped, staring ahead into the gloom.

"Wind's wrong," he said, looking at Kubla. "Too much snow."

He turned into the wind and went back to the cabin.

The fire was low now, concentrated on the heavy roof

timbers and what was left of the walls. He decided to throw some water on the flames but found no bucket.

"Must've been inside," he muttered, defeated.

He noticed then that Dalziel's barrel of aviation fuel was gone, and understood, suddenly, more of what must have happened. He returned to the cache and, seeing that it was uncovered, removed his snowshoes and climbed the ladder for a look.

The pelts were gone, along with the food bags. Some of the moose was still there.

He looked back at the fire.

It was too late to do anything, and now he was too tired to even think. He reached into the cache and threw a bundled moosehide onto the ground, then descended and removed the packs from Kubla, carrying them up to the cache and covering them with the tarp. He dragged the hide under some clustered, low-boughed spruce, where he flattened a place in the snow, first with his snowshoes on and then with them off. In the flat spot, he spread the hide and placed his eiderdown on top. He stuffed the pack and his snowshoes under one of the trees, climbed fully clothed into the eiderdown and rolled himself up in the moosehide, drawing part of it over his head. His rifle went at the edge of the hide, covered but away from the warmth of his body.

Someone will pay for this, he thought. And I'm the one who'll collect.

3

M A N Y   H O U R S   L A T E R and a dozen miles north of the trapline, Wade drew Joe's toboggan into an alcove in a small canyon that ran along a creek. He'd been following the creek up from the South Nahanni River toward the big lake that the pilot, George Dalziel, had referred to as Glacier Lake. It was shadowed by granite peaks to the west, and surrounded by heavily forested slopes to the south and north. His cabin was at the east end of this lake, and too far away for tonight.

In the alcove was a lean-to, hard against the canyon wall, fresh snow sprinkled on its spruce-bough floor and piled a foot deep on its canvas cover. Wade kicked some mounds on the ground in front of the lean-to, revealing a pile of firewood and two crossed logs. He used his foot to clear the fresh snow away from the logs and downed his backpack. Pulling some dry, moss-covered spruce branches from the back end of the lean-to, he stuffed them where the logs crossed.

He reached into his pocket, pulled out the cigarette lighter and flicked it with his thumb. It flared brightly and ignited the branches. He watched the fire spread for a minute, then placed some larger pieces of spruce on it. Then he examined the lighter in the fire's glow, turning it over and over in his hands.

"Scotsman," he said, studying the decoration on the lighter, an embossed likeness of a jaunty man in a kilt. "Saw plenty of them die."

He tried to remember the name of the regiment, but all that came was a vision of kilted corpses scattered across the mud for as far as you could see, thick as leaves in autumn. Someone had made a path through them for the advancing Canadians, so the bodies along the path were especially numerous and arranged more systematically, some even propped theatrically against one another, as if they were conversing or about to stand up and salute.

Mumbling, Wade returned the lighter to his pocket and unstrapped his eiderdown, spreading it over the spruce boughs in the lean-to. He made tea in his billy and sat hunched over the fire, his hands lovingly cradling the cup. As he sipped from it, his eyes darted nervously from the opening in the alcove to another opening in the cliff opposite, over the creek.

They'd stay away from him now, wouldn't have expected him to find one of their cabins.

He finished his tea and, without removing his moccasins or any of his clothes, rolled into his eiderdown.

Sleep came instantly, but was disturbed by distant explosions, as if the one he'd caused was echoing along the bluff. He saw orange and yellow flashes in the dark, and fires with shadowy figures moving around them. His nose stung with cordite. His chest seized up and he couldn't breathe. With a thrash he jerked awake and sat up, breathing hard.

It was the old dream that he could never shake, that made him fear sleep.

The cold began to penetrate, and he saw that his fire had burned down to embers. Pushing his eiderdown back, he stood up and straddled one of his fire logs, lifting it forward. Then he swung around and straddled the other, butting it up against the first.

He returned to his eiderdown and drifted off again as the fire began to crackle. This time he dreamed faces, dirt-streaked and fearful, illuminated by the flashes and fires. A row of prisoners was huddled against the sand-bagged bulwark of a machine-gun nest, facing two guards with bayoneted rifles and listening to voices arguing a short distance away.

"*Verfluchte schweine! Hunde!*"

A figure lurched out of the dark and pointed a pistol. The faces, one of them his, grimaced in fright. An explosion. One of the guards moved to interfere.

The remaining prisoners charged. The guards were overwhelmed in a rain of fists, boots and finally bullets, though two more prisoners were hit at point-blank range by pistol fire.

"Let's get out of here," one of the prisoners whispered, taking a rifle from a dead guard.

"The others'll be here any minute!"

"Get the pistols."

Seconds later, three of the prisoners clambered over the embankment and disappeared into the dark. Another crawled after them, clutching his side, then slumped to the ground.

4

EPPLER AWAKENED WITH a start, pushing the moosehide back and sitting upright. A few feet away, Kubla's great shaggy head, capped with white, popped up. Snow was still falling, moderately now, and not driven by wind. He thought, I've been dreaming, but as soon as he looked around he knew he had not dreamt. He heaved the hide off, seized his rifle, opened the lever partway, glanced into the chamber, closed the lever and stood up, brushing aside the snow-laden branches of the spruce he'd hidden beneath. Slinging the rifle over his shoulder, he shook out the eiderdown and the tarp, rolled the eiderdown into the tarp and stuck the bundle under the moosehide. He strapped on his snowshoes and made straight for the cabin, Kubla following.

It was a sad sight in the early dawn, with only the bottom round of logs left, and those burned through in places and pushed out at the corners. Some of the upper logs had been blown outward at crazy angles; they had a dusting of snow on them, but the centre of the cabin was entirely clear, the ground damp and steaming. Eppler removed his snowshoes and stepped into the empty space. He began to search through the ashes in the area where the door had been, keeping his rifle close at hand as he worked and regularly glancing up and around. He found, as he expected, chunks of melted metal, the remains of the fuel barrel. These he tossed one by one against the bottom round of logs. There were no bones. He was relieved, but not greatly. The fire was too hot, he reasoned. There would be no human remains.

He soon stopped, stood up and looked around, noticing, at the edge of the clearing, what looked like a stick protruding from the snow. Shouldering his rifle, he waded over and pulled at it. It moved, but not easily. He scooped snow off it. It was the door and part of the door frame. He heaved it up onto the snow and dragged it over to the cabin, propping it on one of the scattered logs. It showed no sign of any burning.

"Blown right off."

In the frame, he found a hole, clean on the outside part of the frame, shattered wood on the inside.

He sat on the remains of the wall. Kubla came up to him and sat close.

"I figure Joe's been murdered," he concluded, reaching out to stroke the dog. "And Ghengis too. They've both been burnt, and the furs stolen."

He thought for a while longer.

"But why the hell ... ? A few hundred bucks' worth of pelts?"

He thought that what he really should do, and right away, was head south, down the South Nahanni, over a ridge to the west that Dal had pointed out from the plane, and onto Irvine Creek, which flowed into the Flat River near Albert Faille's cabin. That trip would take two weeks or more, carrying him past the middle of April.

It was at Faille's, at the end of April, that the Flat River trappers and prospectors congregated to play cards and spin stories until the ice started to move out. Usually it took less than a week to get down the Flat, through the canyons and splits of the South Nahanni, into the wide sweep of the Liard River and then into the Mackenzie River. Just north of where the Liard met the Mackenzie was Fort Simpson.

Simpson had an RCMP post, but by the time the police started a search, the killer would be long gone.

"They'll suspect me, Kubla. Never should have told anyone that story about myself."

And what if Joe was, somehow, alive and in trouble?

Eppler figured he had a clear month to search, before the creeks and rivers would start to run, and movement would be difficult if not impossible.

He stood up.

"We're gonna find who did this, Kubla. He's gotta be around here. He won't keep going north unless he's crazy. We're gonna get him down to Simpson. If he kills us, we tried. We played our hand."

Through the morning, he prepared to move, strapping the packs on Kubla, loading a bag of moose cuts—the only food left in the cache—and then going back to the toboggan that he'd abandoned in the swamp. There, where he felt safer than he did around the cabin, he lit a fire, made tea in his billy and fried some of the moose for himself and Kubla. The frozen corpses of his previous day's catch he simply tossed off the trail into the bush.

As he watched Kubla eating the moose, Eppler remembered that this was Joe's first moose. His partner had shot it about a month ago, when they were just finishing up the previous moose, and was sure proud of his accomplishment. Even if the moose did almost walk right into the cabin and lay himself on the table.

Later in the afternoon, back at the cache, Eppler collected the eiderdown, the canvas and the hide. Then he loaded the toboggan and his pack.

He would soon be out of food. All he had for rice, tea

and tobacco was what he'd been carrying when he worked the trapline. But he knew where he could stock up. Dalziel had pointed out the location of his other line in the area, on the right bank of the Nahanni about two miles downstream from the hotsprings. "In case of an emergency," he'd said. "There's some rice, prunes and maybe tea there."

By noon Eppler was heading north. The snow had almost stopped, and the sky was once again a solid, low-hanging blanket of cloud.

5

JUST A HUNDRED miles south as the crow flies, their camps strung out along the Flat River and on adjacent lakes and streams, Eppler's neighbours were coming through the winter in more ordinary ways. Closest, near the mouth of Irvine Creek, was Albert Faille, who, with a decade of trapping experience in the area up the Nahanni and along the Flat, had the most seniority. Thirty miles downstream from him, at the junction of the Flat and Caribou rivers, were the pilot George Dalziel's partner, Nazar Zenchuk, and a newcomer from Yellowknife, John Lomar, hired by Dalziel to help Zenchuk. Both Dalziel and Zenchuk had been in and out of the area for five years; their line was now being worked after lying fallow through the previous winter. Thirty miles up the Flat from Faille were two sets of prospecting partners working adjacent creeks that flowed north into the Flat: Gus Kraus and Bill Clark on Bennett Creek and Milt Campbell and Harry

Vandaele on McLeod Creek. Of the prospectors, only Clark had been around longer than Faille. He was well established, with financial backers in Edmonton, and he and Kraus normally flew in and out of the area from their base at McMillan Lake. Vandaele and Campbell, like the trappers, usually used a scow to come up the Nahanni and the Flat onto McLeod Creek.

Faille was having the most "fun," as he liked to call it, having just started to see again after a bout of snow blindness. He'd tracked an insomniac grizzly, which had left his prints across the trapline, up Irvine Creek and was bringing bags of fat and a giant pelt back to his camp when he went blind. He'd ignored the headaches and his itchy, weepy eyes until it was too late.

By the time he realized what was happening, he was still about five miles from home. He tore the sleeve off his shirt and blindfolded himself to stop the irritation. His eyes felt as though they were stuffed with gravel. "Blindman's bluff, Albert," he muttered. "And you better not miss."

He managed to find a short piece of rope and attach it to the back of the sled. He wrapped the other end around his wrist a couple of times, hoisted his pack, slung his rifle over his shoulder and told his dogs to mush.

"Take me home, boys."

He had to stop and right the sled when it tipped, which was often. A few times he tripped over it and bags that had fallen off.

"Good idea, Albert. Fall down. Stumble around. Wolves'll be right over to see what's up. 'Where are you going, little man?'"

Once he lost his grip on the rope. He yelled at the dogs to stop, got up and began running after them, only to flip head-first over the sled. The dogs had stopped instantly.

"Regular circus act. The wolves are laughing so hard they've changed their minds about eating me. Good thing, too. Rifle's likely plugged with snow by now."

He knotted the rope onto his wrist and kept going, chatting away to himself and his dogs. Later, he rolled down a steep bank onto some ice, finding himself tangled in the straps with the sled and the dogs. While sorting that out, he realized he was on the Flat River. He found the axe, took his rope off the sled and made his way up the line of dogs.

With the rope tied to the lead dog and around his waist, he advanced step by careful step, chopping as he went, the dogs whining and howling for home and crowding up behind him so he had to flail out with the flat of the axe to make them keep their distance. He was wary of overflows, where thin ice covered water gushing from a crack in the thicker ice below.

Finally he reached the other side and felt his way to a gentle slope up onto the riverbank. He went around to the back of the sled and ordered his dogs to mush.

"Stop at our cabin, boys. I don't want to visit Gus. It's too far, and once we eat all the bear fat, I'll be hungry enough to make my way up the harness with my knife between my teeth, lookin' for some leg of canine, some haunch of husky."

At his cabin he got a fire going, stumbled up to the cache to store the hide and fat, fed the dogs and gathered willow twigs. He drank as much willow tea as he could to ease the headache.

"Wonder where Bill got those sunglasses?" he said as he drifted into a long sleep.

Late the next morning, groping for the woodpile, he ended up lost in the woods behind it, colliding with trees. He crawled back through the snow, reaching out to feel for the woodpile, for his chopping block and sawhorse, for the log block seats around the fire ring in the clearing in front of the cabin. After that, he found a rope hanging by the cabin door, tied one end to the door and one around his waist, and for a week used the rope whenever he went out. By the time the blizzard hit, he could see again, but not well. All in all, it had been three weeks since he'd last worked his line.

"Wolverines were eating all my catch. Wolves too, dining out at Albert's Café."

Meanwhile Lomar, down the river, had been hard at work, covering both his and Zenchuk's parts of the line, and was cleaning hides when the blizzard struck. Zenchuk had left the week before, with Dalziel, to fly out the hides and check another line on the Hyland River in the Yukon.

Up the Flat from Faille, Kraus was alone too, Clark having flown out a couple of weeks earlier from their main camp on McMillan Lake. He'd been picked up by one of their backers, the pilot Wop May, and was off to Edmonton to meet other members of what he had named the Liard-Nahanni Syndicate, to tell them how the prospecting was going on Bennett Creek.

After saying goodbye to Clark and May, Kraus had headed over to the creek. He was lighting fires in the hole to thaw it, then widening it and taking it down to bedrock, lugging the sand, gravel and stones in a bucket up a ladder. Once out of the hole he pulled out the stones and threw them onto one pile, then dumped the sand and gravel in another pile for sluicing in the spring.

His main concern, as he worked, was meat. As soon as he'd arrived back on the creek, he'd been lucky enough to encounter a cow moose and her calf on their way past the hole. He fetched his rifle while they ran upstream. He blasted off four shots at their bouncing rears, hoping to hobble them before they got too far, but nothing happened except they ran faster and disappeared around a bend. He raced for the bend, certain they'd be down, but there was no sign of any moose, and no blood on the snow anywhere. He walked back to his hole, shaking his head.

A couple of days later, as he lugged a bucket of rocks up the ladder, it occurred to him that he'd fallen down the creekbank on his way from the lake. He'd managed to keep hold of his rifle, but the adjustable sights might have hit something. If that wasn't it, he was going blind. He immediately nailed an old tin can to a nearby tree, crossed to the other side of the creek, took careful aim and fired. When he went over to look, he saw no mark on the tree. He tried again, aiming low this time, grazing the tree a clear eight inches above the tin. Cursing, he reset his sights, using four more valuable shells, and then went hunting down toward the Flat.

He came back the next day, after an unsuccessful stalk and an uncomfortable night dozing under a spruce tree. Finally, about a half-mile from his hole, he bagged a ptarmigan. He carried it back to the hole, lit a fire, stuck the bird on a stick and rotated it in the flames, burning the feathers off, eating the cooked meat around the outside and then cooking more and eating that. He was halfway through the ptarmigan and a long speech concerning his lousy luck when suddenly he stood up, sniffed the wind, looked at the sky and cursed again. He tossed the ptarmigan aside, threw his pick and shovels into the hole, packed up his lean-to and loped away up the creek.

Five hours later he crashed into his house tent at McMillan Lake in a swirl of snow. I'll stay in bed for a week, he thought. Give my luck some time to change.

A few miles east, Vandaele and Campbell were hard at a game of cards and a bottle of Governor General's rum when the blizzard hit. They were holidaying, because Vandaele had had an accident down on the creek and had agreed to a period of recuperation to, as he put it, "settle his nerves."

A couple of days earlier he'd left work in their hole on McLeod Creek to get meat. Down on the Flat he'd tracked and found a cow moose and her yearling calf. Having them at close range, he'd lifted his Ross rifle and fired.

The next thing he knew, he was on his back in the snow, staring up at the milky sky. He could taste blood and feel it cooling on his face. His left arm was numb, fingers unresponsive. He rolled back onto the trail and used his good arm to push himself to his feet.

It seemed that he'd been unconscious for only a minute. He reached for his rifle and examined the barrel; it was split into two parts that were curled back toward the stock, so that the rifle looked more like a crossbow. Handling it, he noted with relief that he was now using his left hand. He headed back to the hole, dazed and shaky, keeping his mind off what could have happened. When he thought of it, he got too weak in the knees to walk.

"Ice in the barrel," Campbell had said when he examined the rifle. "How the hell ... ?"

"I figured it out. I had it slung over my shoulder when we climbed down to shovel out after a burn, so I took it off and leaned it against the side of the hole. It must've warmed up enough to collect condensation later."

"How do you feel?"

"Like a drink."

6

WADE STAYED AT his camp in the canyon for another day and night, and then followed the small creek up to Glacier Lake. All that time, he had a feeling he was being tracked. During his first night back at the lake, he thought he heard dogs barking and rushed out of his cabin, grabbing the ammo pack and rifle from their pegs on the wall just outside the door. He'd long ago prepared a blind, one of three nearby, on a small bluff that had a hollow near the top. Anyone coming from above would go around the bluff and end up between him and the cabin. Anyone coming down the lake or up the creek would be visible as long as there was enough light.

He waited for a couple of hours, until the cold made

it impossible to stay still. Then he circled. No tracks, no sounds, but the feeling didn't go away. He was spooked by everything—the swish of a load of snow falling off a spruce branch, the chortle of a passing raven.

The isolation wasn't working as he'd hoped. The pilot had said he'd be a hundred miles from the nearest people. Not even the Indians go through there anymore, he'd said. A bloody lie. There was someone just a couple of days away. Judging by the fuel barrel, the dead man had been working one of the pilot's own lines!

Now that he had pelts, maybe he could buy a ride out when the pilot turned up with supplies. He could claim he'd gotten sick and gathered up the traps. No. The pilot would probably be heading for Simpson, where there'd be some curious police, or he'd be dropping in on the guy at the lake below, looking to deliver more supplies and maybe gas up his plane. Once he saw the cabin, he'd get suspicious.

Better to shoot the pilot when he arrived with the groceries, and hit the trail. There'd be enough food and tobacco for another couple of months at least. On the move he'd feel safer, could change direction at a whim, cover different distances each day, surprise his pursuers, walk right up to them and kill them.

Alf and Marty should've thought like that. The morning after the three of them got away from the machine-gun nest, a woodcutter stumbled on them while they were trying to figure out where to penetrate the German lines and get back to their own side. Alf thought they should wait for an attack; one was planned soon, and in the chaos they might just make it. Marty argued that it could be weeks before another attack. You couldn't judge by the weather; it also depended on the intelligence reports. They should try right away while the Germans were still scrambled.

The woodcutter walked right up to them, said something like a greeting and walked on past. Alf and Marty objected when he'd moved to shoot the man down, saying it was too noisy, that they couldn't just shoot an unarmed man in cold blood and that if they killed civilians and the Germans did get them, they'd be dead for sure.

Fools. A couple of hours later, a half-dozen soldiers came, with dogs. He'd already convinced Alf and Marty that they'd split up if they had to run. Maybe then at least one would get back to tell their story. When he heard the shooting start behind him, he doubled back, got the dogs and two of the Germans just after they'd finished off Alf and Marty. He knew the other Germans would go back, not chance it without dogs.

Later, when he was hiding in an empty root cellar, a woman and a kid found him. It was only afterwards, in the field hospital, that he remembered the surprised looks on their faces when he slit their throats. But he was quick; there was no time for them to get frightened.

The dreams started in the hospital. They were giving him pills and shots, keeping him asleep. But when he was asleep he was at the front, a circle of faces around a flickering candle while the air outside screamed and the ground shook and sent dirt down on them until the faces started muttering and crying. Or he was with Alf and Marty, or after.

The dreams didn't stop when they transferred him back

to Canada, or later when he got out of the hospital. Someone was still tracking him, trying to find him. He heard the voices. He saw them. He found their half-smoked cigarettes, footprints, food crumbs.

He'd run into one of them on the Beaver River, just before he met Dalziel and his partner on the Coal River. Said he was a trapper and a prospector, talked on in a funny accent about the Klondike, and then some place called Bullion Creek near a big lake, and then Atlin. His name was strange, Shyback or something, and his cabin was too clean. Even his fingernails were clean! Led the conversation around to the war, asked about the Ross rifle and the pistol, saying he knew now it was true that you got to keep your weapons after the war. Made the mistake of reaching for the rifle, pretending he just wanted to look at it.

7

THREE HUNDRED MILES south, at Fort Simpson, George Dalziel sat staring at Dr. Truesdell, who served as the magistrate, medical officer and Indian agent, all officialdom rolled into one. Truesdell, one hand propping his head, pushing up his long, iron-grey hair, was poring over his papers. This went on for some time—Dalziel staring, Truesdell reading and fussing with his papers. Then Truesdell dropped his hand, lifted his head and, over the top of his reading glasses, aimed what he probably meant to be a penetrating glance at Dalziel.

Like a teacher, Dalziel thought, trying to keep the sarcastic look off his face, a look that had got him into trouble when he was a kid, at home and at school. In fact, Truesdell always reminded him of the teachers at his private school in Vancouver, a bunch of intellectual eunuchs, pompous Brit know-it-alls. Even among boys they were out of their depth, fond of proselytizing about Shakespeare, Byron etc., men with whom they had nothing whatsoever in common, whose lives and accomplishments were a rebuke. Truesdell was hoping to induce talk. Dalziel intended to disappoint him.

Dalziel knew that with the purchase of his Curtiss Robin and use of it for trapping, he'd become a headache for Truesdell. Now, the good doctor was probably going to show him how much of a headache.

Finally, Truesdell cleared his throat and said, "If Corporal Newton told you to proceed until he could get a clear legal opinion, I'm afraid he was creating confusion where there is none."

The words echoed in the dusky office, lit only by a couple of Aladdin lamps that were roaring softly, one on Truesdell's desk and the other on a wall bracket behind it.

"Not *if*. He told me to proceed."

"Verbally?"

"We're not pen pals. He told me to go ahead and catch them and to bring them in and he'd issue a licence for that many. I brought in six."

"The regulations are clear. It says here that you need a special licence to trap wild animals for the purpose of breeding them."

"I was trapping them for sale."

"To a breeder. I think the law is clear, Dal."

"The corporal didn't think so."

"But I do, and that's why I have to order Newton to prepare charges. I'll have to tell Vera Turner to keep the marten a while longer as evidence."

"They're dead," said Dalziel, getting up to leave.

Truesdell looked surprised, but lifted a finger. "I have something else to discuss with you."

Dalziel stood waiting, examining the calendar on the wall behind Truesdell. March 1936, the Houses of Parliament in Ottawa on a clear day, Union Jack flying from the central tower.

"Are you flying to Edmonton once the weather breaks?"

Dalziel shrugged.

"I have a patient, an Indian woman, who needs to get to Edmonton as soon as possible. Appendicitis. I could do the operation myself, of course, but I'd need assistance and the Gray Nuns aren't trained for that. Mackenzie Air and Canadian have stopped flying, and even after the weather clears they'll be a couple of days getting here."

"How bad is she?"

"She'll be all right for a few more days. I can give you a cheque for her fare if you tell me how much."

"Sixty dollars. That's my gas money. And I'll need a note certifying that I'm flying a sick passenger in an emergency. For some reason, the Department of Transport is keeping an eye on me. I'll get the note and the cheque when I pick up your patient."

"I appreciate that, but I can send someone with it. Where are you staying?"

But even as Truesdell asked, Dalziel had turned and was walking out of the room. Truesdell watched him, sighed deeply and returned to his papers. There was a gust of air and then the outside door closed.

8

DALZIEL KNELT AND strapped on his snowshoes. He could hear laughter off to his right, someone coming out of the Hudson's Bay store maybe, or Northern Traders, or Whittington's hotel, café and bar farther down the road. The government compound—which included RCMP headquarters, the hospital, the wireless station, the experimental farm and the Indian office—looked over the rest of the town, which occupied most of a small island in the Mackenzie River. The only thing above the compound was Truesdell's house. The road ran from there south, past the Anglican and Catholic churches and the store, the Commercial Bank and Whittington's, and then down to the Indian treaty area at the island's southern tip. There, a dozen large tents and a few shacks sat on 20 acres that sloped down to the shallow channel of the river between Fort Simpson and the mainland.

Dalziel headed northeast, on a path that ran around Truesdell's house, over the island's hump and past Albert Faille's cabin to the river. As he walked he could look over the line of stunted spruce and willow along the shore, and see the vast expanse of the Mackenzie River, distinguishable from the land only because of its flatness. The opposite shore was a good mile away, imperceptible in the blowing snow.

The trail came to a steep bank, dropping 50 feet to the river, and then turned and meandered through the bush along the edge of the bank. In an open space, Dalziel stood for a moment in the wind. He was thinking about Truesdell and his little local enterprises. The doctor had a market garden that produced vegetables for missions along the Mackenzie River up to Aklavik, and some pastures along the shore where he grew oats and hay for local livestock. He also filled firewood contracts for the government buildings and riverboats, a conflict of interest if there ever was one, since Truesdell also did the purchasing. He was not a popular employer; the people he hired got less than they expected and waited too long for their pay. They groused in the café or hotel but were too intimidated to complain. Who wants to cross the magistrate and doctor?

Dalziel resumed walking. Soon he arrived at a tent suburb. The tents were the residences of white trappers and prospectors who came to town on business and spent their summers there, and of new arrivals who'd be out now looking for work. In winter, the trappers of Simpson, white and Indian, drove dogs or snowshoed along the Liard and Mackenzie between their lines and town. New tents were going up all the time and the trails on the rivers were packed from continual use, because the country was filling up with men from the south, driven off their farms by drought and the Depression.

Word had got out about the money in fur. Rich people in the south were richer now, if only because the poor were poorer and charging less for their services. Dalziel was aware of that equation and not interested in being on the wrong side of it.

And even more attractive than trapping, which was hard work, was the promise of gold, though so far none had been found. Gold prices had reached an all-time high, and legends had grown about the Nahanni region, about a lost mine discovered by three brothers, Willie, Frank and Charlie McLeod, the half-breed sons of the Hudson's Bay Company factor at Fort Liard.

The McLeods, the story went, had long heard from the Indians about a gold find along the Flat River near the Yukon border, and in the winter of 1904 they hit the trail to check out the rumours. They started, God knows why, in Vancouver, and went by steamer up the Inside Passage to Wrangell in the Alaska Panhandle, by dog team up the frozen Stikine River to Telegraph Creek, Dease Lake and the Liard River, then farther north up the Hyland River—fighting spring blizzards (the story usually went), so it was 1905 now—and over the divide into the headwaters of the Flat River. Not far down the Flat they found some Indians who were sluicing on a creek and getting coarse gold. The McLeods joined them, filled a medicine bottle with gold, converted a couple of whip-sawed sluice boxes into a scow and headed for home down the Flat River. The scow broke up in the Flat River Canyon and the medicine bottle was lost, but the brothers salvaged the planks, built a new scow and continued on down the Flat into the South Nahanni and out onto the Liard, arriving home with nothing to show for their adventures but a damned good story about a gold strike.

A year later, Willie and Frank went back up the Nahanni to refind the mine, taking a Scotsman (in one version of the story he was also a mining engineer) named Weir with them. A year went by with no word, so Charlie set out, in the summer of 1907, to track the little party. It hadn't gone far. He found his brothers in what came to be known as Deadmen Valley, between First and Second Canyon of the Nahanni. He recognized the skeletons from their gear. In various stories they were tied to trees and headless, or merely headless, or headless and just out of their eiderdowns and reaching for their rifles. In all versions there was a message scrawled in charcoal on a tree blaze: "We have found a fine prospect."

Another year later, another headless body was found by Indians, upstream from the McLeods' last camp. It was assumed by police to be Weir, but Charlie believed Weir had actually murdered his brothers and departed the country with their gold and the secret of its source. Charlie started looking for Weir.

This story meshed with, or was dreamed up with an eye to, an earlier story told by Indians to the early explorers and subsequently much embellished by those explorers, about headhunting (or cannibalistic) Indians living above the falls in a tropical valley. These Indians were supposed to be exceedingly possessive of their turf; they killed any and all intruders.

But that didn't stop anyone. Dalziel broke into an abrupt laugh. Hell, that was an attraction. If you couldn't make a living you could at least have an adventure. The wilder the stories got, the more the southern newspapers retold them, adding their own elaborations, and the more men turned up to check things out. Their attitude seemed to be that if you didn't have an adventure, exactly, you'd certainly have the material for making one up.

A couple of Dalziel's customers, Harry Vandaele and Milt Campbell, were looking for the lost mine right now, having gone home to their families for Christmas and returned earlier than usual to work their hole on McLeod Creek. Gus Kraus and Bill Clark had been at it for three years, on McLeod, Borden and Bennet creeks. Albert Faille had started his search a decade ago—going above the falls year after year and coming out with his head in place, though Dalziel was starting to wonder about that. Almost certainly they were all wasting their time.

Truesdell spent some of his well-paid working hours firing letters off to the *Edmonton Journal,* trying to stop all those "damn fool articles," as he called them, and stem the tide of whites. Not a chance. The articles sold thousands of papers. It was all straight out of H. Ryder Haggard, Dalziel's father's favourite author and, for a time, his own: Zulu ghosts, now Indian ghosts and guardian spirits, and jungle valleys heated here by hotsprings.

Mad trappers, a truly local embellishment.

Mad *flying* trappers. Dal's operation, the first of its kind, had attracted the attention of the newspaper in Edmonton, where he lived. He'd even made it into the *New York Times.*

The men he flew in always asked, "Did you go looking for the mine? Is there gold in this Nahanni country?"

All except Wade, the latest, whom he'd planted at Glacier Lake in November last year, the farthest in he'd ever taken anyone. Wade hadn't asked a thing, hadn't *said* a thing.

Which, Dalziel recalled, he'd deeply appreciated at the time, his mind on an offer of $500 each for live, healthy marten for breeding. Catching the marten was as hard as teaching a dog to walk on its hind legs, but he finally did it, on a lake just north of where he'd dropped Wade. Caught them without hurting them, caged them and flew them 300 miles. Only to have Corporal Newton turn up, while he and Vera Turner were figuring out how to feed them, with the news that Truesdell had objections.

A month of careful work gone for nothing.

9

TRUESDELL, STUFFING HIS cheque and note of permission for Dalziel into an envelope, heard Newton moving around, got up, opened the door between their two offices and beckoned him in.

Newton was young and still full of his barracks-room training: his uniform neat, his hair and mustache trimmed, his walk brisk. He knew his duties well but was unfamiliar with the north, a fact that worried Truesdell, who was himself putting in his fourth year as medical officer, Indian agent and magistrate. Newton still needed a guide to do his river patrols, and that was expensive. Soon he would get familiar with the dogs, sleds, scows and snowshoes, and then he would be

· 34 ·

moved elsewhere. Truesdell, however, had to admit that even though Newton was green he learned quickly, wore his authority well and dealt with the locals easily. Even the Indians would sometimes joke with him.

"Dal's flying Mary out as soon as the snow stops. I'm giving him a note saying it's a mercy flight."

"He asked for it?"

"I thought it was a good idea."

"I guess so. Considering how many times you've complained to Transport about him."

"I told him you were going to lay charges in connection with the marten."

"I am?"

"He drove me to it. Looks like a clear case to me."

"It's not a clear case, and it especially won't be clear when his lawyer gets through with it. I *did* tell him to proceed and I don't intend to lie about that."

"Most damnable uncommunicative man I've ever encountered!"

"No money in talk," said Newton. "Seriously, you've tried before to shut him down on minor violations, and it didn't work. It won't work this time, either, and he knows it."

"It'll help keep him honest."

"Maybe he *is* honest."

"Good lord, Regis. He's hauling a fortune in furs out of this country. I heard that his last shipment to Edmonton was worth $5,000, and that was only his first load for the winter. How much do you get paid in a year?"

"Five hundred dollars, as you well know. But there's no

law against making money and he's bloody good at what he's doing. He made plenty even when he was on foot. Toughest man I've ever met, actually, and people say he knows the area as well as Faille does. You know he crossed that whole Nahanni country on foot one summer, from Upper Post to Fort Norman?"

"I've heard all that, Regis. It's an old story."

"It says plenty about the man and about how he's regarded in this country. Six weeks was all it took him. Inconceivable!"

"He wasn't doing anything heroic, Regis. He was just looking for trapping areas that are away from the Liard and Mackenzie, places where he could cream off marten with no bother. He's made a specialty of intruding on areas in the backcountry, where the Indians are still free of white interference and can trap on the move, like they always did. Only Faille was in there regularly, and he was accepted as an oddity. But then Dalziel started trapping on the move, taking the best spots, and then he got that damned plane and started putting permanent lines and men at those spots. When the Indians come across his lines or find him occupying their cabins, he tells them, in no uncertain terms, to bugger off. Some of them have given up trying to compete, and stay around town picking up pogey."

"But there's nothing illegal about what he's doing."

"The government has to change that, and not just for the sake of the Indians. Most of his shipments go to Edmonton instead of the local trading posts. Then there's the men he brings in. They get only fifty percent of the take, less if they're inexperienced, and some have come out no better than when they went in. I've given a couple of them work clearing land so they could earn their fare out of here."

"Still, it's mighty handy to have a plane based here, wouldn't you say? Good for the Indians as well as for us."

Truesdell shifted uncomfortably. "Not at the price. He's already brought in one of his hired men, dead."

"That was Nazar's cousin and he had a heart attack, as you yourself certified."

"More could die. Dalziel doesn't look too closely into how healthy his employees happen to be. And he doesn't check on them that regularly, either. The cousin was on a line 20 miles away from Nazar, and God knows where Dal was at the time."

"They could limit the number of assistants."

"That's one of the suggestions we've made. Crerar tells me he's almost ready to put some new regulations before Parliament. I've convinced him that something has to be done. In that sense, Dalziel and his plane have been a blessing because the issue is being forced. But meanwhile, we need to limit the damage. We need to ground Dalziel. Are you sure we have nothing to go on with the live marten he brought in?"

"As I see it, he hasn't broken the law—he's just gone beyond it. I say fine him."

"That won't stop him. We should've hit him with a criminal offence when he raided Clark and Kraus's cache a couple of years ago. We missed our chance there."

"Even that was a minor infraction, nothing to lay a charge on. Dalziel apologized on the spot and paid for the damage."

Truesdell sighed. "Another fine, then."

"What? A hundred dollars?"

"That's the usual."

"He won't challenge it. It'd cost him more in lawyer's fees. He'll pay it."

"Of course he will. It's nothing to him."

"It's something to us. When he pays, we don't look like *complete* idiots."

10

THAT AFTERNOON, UP at Glacier Lake, Wade was in the bush at the back of his cabin, frantically chopping and sawing a hole through the bottom three rounds of the wall. People had been messing with his ammo and equipment while he slept. The pistol he kept fully loaded and beside his bed—one shell was gone from its chamber this morning. A few days ago, his coat pocket was empty when he went out and grabbed the rifle from under the eaves, fishing for a shell to plug into the chamber. And the knife he'd put in the blind along the south shore of the lake was gone.

He wanted desperately to leave, to get on the move, but he needed the supplies that the pilot had promised.

The hole would be a way out of the cabin into thick bush. When he finished cutting it, he'd fit chunks of firewood into it and caulk them with dampened floor dirt. The dirt would freeze instantly, holding the firewood in place and making the wall look solid. Next time he heard them close to the cabin, he'd kick the firewood out and slip through. The .22

would go behind a board under the back eaves, and he'd be able to come around the cabin and ambush them. They'd been getting closer since he'd arrived. That's why he hadn't been able to trap. Now they were coming right in, the doctors and nurses from the hospital, wanting him to talk, tell them things. They even brought in his mother once. His jaw was sore and his mouth raw from the shocks they gave him, and he was so tired some mornings that he couldn't get out of bed until noon, until it got so cold in the cabin that he had to move.

Sometimes he could wake himself up when they came, but usually he couldn't. Or he was awake but couldn't move. He'd hear their voices outside, talking about him—what drugs they were going to give him, where they were going to put him. He'd try to heave himself up but hadn't the strength, as if there was a weight on his chest. Then they would come to get him.

Next time they came, he would know what to do.

11

DALZIEL STRODE ALONG the bluffs above the Mackenzie River, and turned toward one of the tents. As he approached it, the gigantic heads of a half-dozen huskies emerged from the drifts, but the dogs recognized Dalziel and lay down again. He stopped in front of the door of the tent and glanced at the river. Through a gap in the willows and spruce he could see the Robin sitting not far offshore.

It looked small, fragile, insignificant, almost blotted out by the swirling snow. A canvas bonnet covered the plane's engine and extended down to the snow, and guy ropes were attached to the posts of a pier now frozen into the ice. Nearby fuel barrels were topped with humps of snow.

With luck, the storm would end tomorrow, and he could get to Edmonton to pick up a hunting party. Up here, lately, he was going nowhere.

Dalziel untied and lifted a flap, ducked his head and stepped into the tent.

On either side, a narrow bed covered with an eiderdown sleeping bag. In back, some shelves. In front of the shelves an airtight heater, glowing red, with a steaming pot on top. In front of the heater a couple of chairs, in one of which sat Nazar Zenchuk, Dalziel's friend and partner since they'd met at Dease Lake six years ago.

Zenchuk was dark-skinned and dark-haired, much taller than Dalziel, with a powerful physique. He had a long, strong face—a prominent chin and a straight, full mouth that was often compressed into a thoughtful frown but that also easily and quickly turned up into a grin. He was grinning now.

"Not in jail yet?"

"Don't worry, they're working on it," said Dalziel, unbuttoning his coat. He pulled it off and threw it on one of the beds.

Zenchuk was still grinning as he stood up, reached over Dalziel and grabbed two tin cups off the shelf. He set the cups on the stove and filled them.

Dalziel took one and sat down. Coffee. Like crankcase oil.

Nazar couldn't live without it. He held the cup in both hands close to his nose but did not drink it, more interested in the heat that was seeping into his hands.

"You're too far ahead of them, Dal. You're too busy. It makes them nervous. Bloody plane coming and going or just flying over to God knows where. It drives them nuts."

"At least they didn't ground the plane."

"Good. You can take me back to the line. I'm getting bored."

"You must be. I figured you'd be at Whittington's."

"I was, but Andy's telling the same old stories to a couple of Indians, trying to get a smile out of them. It's time for me to get back to making money."

"Truesdell wants me to fly one of his patients to Edmonton. That could be *why* we still have the plane."

"That's Mary Littlejohn, Carman's baby sister. He's in the café and he's worried. I could tell because he told me."

"This snow isn't going to last much longer. Probably I'll be at the hospital tomorrow morning, collecting her."

"How much?"

"Sixty dollars."

"Sure as heck there'll be a fare waiting in Edmonton, too, some refugee from a dried-up prairie farm with his last $50 stitched into his woollies, looking for a ride here. Mackenzie Air or Canadian will have laughed him out of their offices, but someone will have told him about the flying trapper."

"I want you to come to Edmonton with me. Lomar can handle the line for another week or two. June always looks forward to seeing you. So does Robin."

"Won't you have a full load with Mary and the pelts?"

"I don't like flying sick or injured people without some-one coming along. What am I supposed to do if she stops breathing? Attend to her or fly the plane? Truesdell wouldn't think about that angle. He just wants to wash his hands of her before she dies on him. So I'd appreciate it if you'd come. We'll sell the bulk of the pelts here when we get back. Jack Mulholland at the Butte will give us a fair price. He likes me since I did him that favour."

"Putting Joe and Bill up at Rabbitkettle?"

"Suggesting it. They paid their fare, 50 bucks each."

"What did you charge them for the line?"

"Ten percent of the take. I know it's not much, but there's no equipment there and no labels on the trees. All I did last fall was leave some fuel, clear a trail and build a cache."

"You coming right back here after Edmonton? Will you fly me in then?"

"I'm hoping for a hunting trip. Just one."

Zenchuk sighed. "Well, Mary's a sweet kid, June's a good cook and Robin's fun to play with. But I don't want to be down there for too long."

"Don't worry. One hunting trip if I get one, and then it's time to check on Wade and put in at Landing Lake until breakup."

"Are you checking on Joe and Bill too?"

"I told you before. No."

"I've been thinking about them. What a crackpot idea that is, coming down the river in a skinboat. Not sturdy enough. If it slides up a rock or hits a wave it's gone, and you're in the river with some sticks and the canvas skin float-ing along beside you and your rifle on the bottom. Eppler's a good man in the bush, they say, but I never heard about him being a boatman. He's always trapped along the Liard. He doesn't know white water. Maybe you should drop in and have a talk with him."

"Look," said Dalziel, leaning forward. "I told them if they couldn't afford to ride out with me they should wait for low water and built a raft. You can't sink a raft. Or better, especially if they want out before the flood's over, they should leave the pelts for me to pick up and walk down past our camp at the Rabbitkettle hotsprings and over to Irvine Creek. Hook up with Faille. I gave them a price of $30 for the pickup."

"Cheap enough."

"Sure. I can fit their hides in with Wade's and whatever I take out of Landing Lake. I won't have to make a special trip. When I flew them in, I showed them the spot to cross over to Irvine Creek. Bill knows you guys will be at Faille's or your camp early in May, and I told him you've got the scow. What more do you want me to do, Nazar? It's up to Bill, and Bill said no."

"You can do me a favour and drop in anyway and argue with him. You'll be flying right over the lake. If you need an excuse, tell him I'm worried. Did you talk to Bill and Joe about Wade?"

"Hell no. I don't want those guys getting together. They got work to do. Bill and Joe are trying to put in a winter's trapping in three months. And I doubt Wade and Eppler would hit it off."

Zenchuk chuckled and sipped his coffee. "You're probably right. He sure as hell made *me* nervous, and I think I'm a lot more understanding than Bill is. Wade knew trapping all right, judging by the questions you asked him, but his equipment was wrong. I wonder if he's using those old moccasins I gave him. And he actually told me he hated dogs. He was scared of ours. You don't work this country without dogs. It's plain stupid."

"I thought the ammo belt was pretty funny," said Dalziel. "It held at least 20 rounds."

"And he never took his hands off his rifle. You don't walk into a man's camp and carry your rifle around with your finger twitching at the safety. I was glad you were around. Maybe I should go with you when you check on him."

"You haven't told anyone about Wade, have you?"

"No."

"Not even Lomar?"

"Lomar and I don't talk."

"Good. Let's keep it quiet until we see how he turns out."

12

THE ROBIN CRUISED at 100 miles per hour, went about 500 miles on its two 25-gallon wing tanks and carried a payload of 450 pounds along with the pilot and a mechanic. Since Dalziel had his mechanic's as well as his pilot's licence, he could add another 150 pounds of payload or passengers.

The plane, with all its limitations, was a daily marvel. He especially felt that when he flew great distances, like now, floating across the white expanse of northern Alberta toward Edmonton. He'd had only a year so far to work out its possibilities and already the plane was earning good money. It had paid for itself, in fact, and the trapping was just a beginning. He was getting more and more inquiries from big-game hunters, wealthy southerners wanting trophies.

The biggest problem so far was Truesdell, or what he represented, and the complex and mercurial body of trapping and transport regulations churned out by Ottawa. So far the transport regulations, prohibiting Dalziel from flying passengers along routes flown by commercial airlines, were the main problem. If a trapper or prospector had $50 and wanted to fly from Edmonton to Fort Simpson, Dalziel was not going to turn him down and head out in an empty plane. Might as well get the gas paid for. If anyone asked, the customer was just a friend.

Except that the RCMP had questioned some of those customers, and their answers must have been evasive or contradictory. Dalziel had already collected two warnings. He'd taken them to a lawyer and learned that there was a difference between gathering evidence and getting testimony in court.

"Right now," the lawyer had said, "they're just fishing. But they *are* fishing."

That had cost $20. But the lawyer was interested in whatever else might come up.

"Most of the time you'll get them off your back just by making them deal with me."

"Don't know if I can afford it."

"The way you operate, you can't *not* afford it."

He was right. And Dalziel knew he was pushing the limits of the law with the trapping operation too. As a licensed trapper, he could have as many lines and hire as many assistants as he wanted, and the supply of disappointed prospectors and hungry refugees from the prairies was endless. He tried to make sure that they at least knew how to hunt. Before he flew them to his lines, he found out as best he could how much time they'd spent outdoors, in the bush, on their own. If they were inexperienced, he spent a few weeks training them on the line, watching to see if they could manage. But he never asked them about their health. What good did it do? Accidents happened all the time, and not even Nazar had known that his cousin had a bad heart. Probably the cousin didn't know.

At least he was making some use of the backcountry. The Indians had more or less abandoned it, tribal skirmishes (with rifles adding efficiency) and influenza epidemics having done for most of them, government pogey slowly killing the rest. On his famous walk to Fort Norman he'd stumbled on the remains of some of their camps, between the Nahanni and the Mackenzie, especially on the eastern ridges of the Mackenzie Mountains. Rotting poles under the moss, with rusted pots, tins and traps. They died in these places and were buried in shallow, crudely fenced graves, and those who were left moved on quickly, carrying what they could.

Now most of them stuck to the Liard and the Mackenzie, huddled around white settlements and trading posts.

He was putting men where the Indians used to be. For the first time, traplines were being worked in the country above the falls. What would those men do after Truesdell forced him out? What would Truesdell and the settlers in Simpson do when his plane wasn't coming and going all the time? What would've happened to Mary Littlejohn, for example?

He looked back. She was asleep in a pile of blankets, cushioned by bundles of pelts.

Nazar, in the passenger seat, snored, matching the engine for volume.

Nearing Edmonton, Dalziel faced the choice between South Cooking Lake, where Mackenzie Air Services and Canadian Airways had new offices, or Blatchford Field right near Edmonton. The lake cost nothing, but MAS and CA had decided that Dalziel was undercutting them, and they made trouble if he pulled in too close to them.

Dalziel decided to put down at Blatchford Field. Mary would get straight to the hospital that way, though it would cost $20 of the $60 that Truesdell had made a show of paying him just as they left Simpson. It would cost time, too. There was bound to be an *Edmonton Journal* reporter lying in ambush, looking for another chapter of the ongoing story. He circled and landed, sliding up through rotting ice and slushy snow to some other private planes about a 15-minute walk from the terminal.

Edmonton was having an early taste of spring. June and the baby would be enjoying it on their daily walks.

It took the guy from the *Journal* exactly 15 minutes to find them.

"How many pelts this time, Dal? Last time it was $5,000 worth, a record. Are you going to break that?"

Dalziel busied himself attaching the engine bonnet. Nazar turned to the reporter.

"Mercy trip this time, Fred."

Oh God, Dalziel thought.

"That's Frank, Nazar. Remember me? Frank Peebles. I wrote that story about Dal that went all the way to the *New York Times*. It's been nominated for a prize in the States. Who's sick?"

"Indian girl. Mary Littlejohn. The medics just picked her up." Zenchuk pointed. "They're heading into the terminal with her."

"Can she talk?"

"Maybe. She was awake when we got here."

Peebles, running backwards, said, "I'll go to the hospital with her. Can I see you both later? How about the coffee shop in the terminal in an hour?"

"How about the bar at the Leland?"

The reporter nodded and turned to catch up to Mary and the medics.

"See Dal? It's easy."

"Mercy flight? I seem to remember charging Truesdell $60."

"Peanuts, and anyway Frank wouldn't use that fact. Not the right angle. And even if he did, he'd bury it. The flying trapper is tough but fair. He has to eat like everyone else. Has a baby boy. Beneath that rough exterior beats a heart of gold." Zenchuk paused for a moment, thinking, and then continued, "As deeply hidden, but as rich, as the lost McLeod Mine."

They both laughed.

"You should be charging for that," Dalziel said.

"I do," said Zenchuk. "At the bar."

13

THE MORNING AFTER he'd touched down in Edmonton, sitting with June over coffee, Robin back to sleep after his Pablum, Dalziel heard the newspaper drop by the apartment door.

"Let's see what Nazar told them this time," said June.

It must've been good, thought Dalziel. Worth a lot of beer. He never made it here last night.

"Front page," said June, placing the *Edmonton Journal* beside Dalziel's cup. Dalziel located the article and read it to her:

DALZIEL AND AIDE FLY MEDICAL EMERGENCY TO EDMONTON

April 3, 1936. Canada's first subarctic trapper to use an airplane arrived in Edmonton yesterday.

Back to civilization, George C. F. Dalziel, 27, the new "mad trapper of the Arctic," as other pilots and trappers have nicknamed him, landed his ski-equipped plane after a trip of more than 1,000 miles from his flying base.

But this was not a business trip. It was the desperate need of 19-year-old Mary Littlejohn that brought Dalziel back to civilization. Doctors at the Edmonton General said Littlejohn arrived just in time, her appendix about to rupture. This is evidence, if more is needed, of the value of air transportation in our empty northland.

Dalziel, aided by his trapping partner Nazar Zenchuk, 30, of Upper Post, has, since mid-September, when he left Edmonton with the plane equipped with floats for landing on open water before the "freeze-up," been flying over his hundreds of miles of traplines.

His base is established on a lake in an unmapped area lying between Fort Simpson on the Mackenzie River and Great Bear Lake to the northeast.

After the "freeze-up," they changed their landing gear to skis, and awaited a chance to fly out with their early winter catch. They left their pontoons "cached" with their extra food supply at the far northern lake.

Their traplines, radiating fan-shaped from their flying base, range from 80 to 100 miles in length. The trappers fly from point to point along the lines, then mush on snowshoes between landing points.

Dressed in heavy parkas, moccasins and other Arctic clothing to withstand the cold weather they experienced before they took off from their flying and trapping base in the Far North, the two young trappers found Edmonton experiencing a mild thaw, with temperatures ranging several degrees above freezing.

Dalziel, a rugged, silent type inured to the Northern trails, left home in Vancouver when 17 years old for a life of adventure in Northern British Columbia and the Yukon.

A few years ago, carrying only a blanket, a rifle and a meagre food supply, he made his way on foot across the mountains from Dease Lake, British Columbia, to Fort Simpson in the Mackenzie Basin. His ability to live off the land while roaming the Northern Wilderness earned him the title of "mystery man" among the natives.

—Frank Peebles

Dalziel looked up to see June beaming at him. Now she'd clip the article and add it to her collection.

"That's wonderful," she said.

He shook his head. "Peebles must be going for another prize. How can he dish out that sort of malarkey?"

"Don't be so modest. Most of it's true. I'm confused about your lake, though. I thought you were at Landing Lake, up the Flat River, not far from Nazar."

"I am. The pontoons are there, so that's where I'll wait for breakup, but Nazar knows not to tell anyone our exact location."

"Only I know?"

"You, Nazar, Lomar and the trappers on the Flat River. Kraus and Clark are there, prospecting. There's a couple of other guys on McLeod Creek. And Faille too, at the mouth of Irvine Creek. It's like a neighbourhood. When the isolation gets to them, they snowshoe 20 miles or more just to play cards and talk. Word gets around."

"Good. And I think you should appreciate what Nazar's doing. He knows you won't tell the reporters anything, and that would mean they'd have to invent it all."

"Which means they might accidentally get it right, and we don't want that. What they need is another Albert Johnson, the original Mad Trapper. They really miss him. He sold millions of papers for them."

"Is Nazar coming to dinner tonight?"

"He said so. He wants to see his godson."

"Are you going to talk to the man about the marten? He's phoned twice."

Dalziel shifted impatiently. "If that little arrangement had worked out, our bank balance would be a lot healthier right now."

"Our balance is fine. I've even sent your sisters their residence money for their next term."

Noises from the adjoining room indicated that the baby was awake again, and June left to attend to him. Dalziel got up, poured himself more coffee and sat down to scan the rest of the paper. He stopped on page 3, at another article about the north:

DEAD TRAPPERS

Fort Liard. Yukon. March 21, 1936. Cst. Winston C. Graham at the Fort Liard detachment was advised by Indian trappers that human remains, evidently those of trapper Andrew Czybek, were found in the wreckage of an isolated cabin near the headwaters of the Beaver River.

The Indians, to whom Cst. Graham refers as being of good repute, found Czybek's cabin burned to the ground, the fire having taken place early in the trapping season. Evidence for this was the fact that only one round of logs was left of the cabin. This is the second death reported in the Liard area this winter. In January, George Dalziel, Edmonton's "flying trapper," brought in the frozen body of Steve Zenchuk. Medical examination indicated that Mr. Zenchuk died of a heart attack.

Dalziel sat staring at the article. Czybek. A Klondiker, one of the originals, retired now but still addicted to the bush, living on a bank account or inheritance or pension. Nazar's closest neighbour last year when he was on the Coal River trapline.

At least his corpse had no connection to the flying, mad, mystery trapper.

Or did it? Wade had turned up at the Coal River camp just about the time Czybek must've died. Czybek's cabin was only two days away from Nazar's.

Dammit. Bill and Joe were only about 25 miles away from Wade.

June came in with Robin and placed him in his arms. As he cuddled the warm, small body he thought, I'll take the dogs with me.

14

THAT AFTERNOON, THE phone rang.

"Mercy flight, Dal? That doesn't sound like you."

It was Harry Snyder, Dalziel's best and most obnoxious customer for guided hunts.

"I've got sides you've never seen, Harry."

"Right now I want the side I like best, the side that needs money. There's a couple of jobs that only you can do for me. I was glad to read in today's paper that you're in Edmonton."

"What do you want done?"

"I bought another Fairchild 71C for the company, a big baby, eight-seater. I want you to take the train back east to Fort Erie, check out the plane, take possession if it's airworthy, supervise repairs if it isn't. I was going to get one of the MAS pilots to do it, but none of them have a mechanic's licence."

"How much?"

"Lemme see. You'll be a week, maybe a bit more. Three hundred dollars, all expenses paid. Or I'll give you twice that in Eldorado shares. You should get into uranium, Dal. It can only go up."

"I'll take the cash."

"Nothing ventured, nothing gained."

"Cash."

"Suit yourself. Now, when you get back, I want a quiet hunt. Three days at most. We'll use the 71C."

"What are you after?"

"*They*. A couple of VIPs. They want Dall sheep, full curl. I'll bring Ross to do the heads. Don't worry, we'll pack them in with half a ton of mining equipment."

"How do we proceed?"

"We'll sort it all out down here at my little teepee. The boys want to meet you, especially after they saw today's paper. I've sent my car. Bring June and the kid—Ida wants to see who married the flying trapper. I'll have you back in Edmonton tomorrow before the train comes in."

He found June in the bedroom, pacing with Robin.

"Take over for a while," June said. "My arms are aching."

Dalziel took Robin, holding him face out and bouncing him. "Let's take him outside," he said. "He likes the air."

"Where to?"

"The park. We have to talk. We're about to go on an outing, to Snyder's, and I want to prepare you."

"He's offering you a job?"

"I'm supposed to pick up a new plane in Fort Erie. It'll take about a week. Then he wants a quiet hunt."

"Quiet?"

"He wants to go somewhere that's not really allowed."

15

A COUPLE OF hours later they were in a beige-and-maroon Packard, heading south to Snyder's "teepee" in Sundre.

"You do anything for Snyder besides drive?" Dalziel asked the chauffeur, who was obviously straight out of some log school, a local, rosy-cheeked, big-eared farm boy who pulled steadily at the knot in his tie as he drove.

"No, but I'm an investor. If I take half my wages in shares, I earn twice as much as I would."

"It might be a gamble."

"No sir. Mr. Snyder's refinanced Eldorado and he has total control. Everything they produce is already sold. The radium is a cancer cure, worth $50,000 an ounce. How does that compare with gold, eh? The uranium goes to the U.S. government for weapons research. Mr. Snyder says there's going to be a war. What do you think uranium will be worth then?"

A hell of a lot more than your life, thought Dalziel.

Snyder's house was a shocking contrast to the grey, disintegrating shacks in the vicinity. From its expansive front porch the Rockies were visible, a jagged row of white, sawtooth peaks that stretched from north to south as far as the eye could see.

Ida Snyder welcomed them at the front door, took immediate possession of Robin and led them to a private suite.

"The butler will come for you at six. He'll bring a maid to watch Robin. She's very good. She raised five kids of her own, so you won't have to worry. There'll be two other guests and their wives, and our daughter Dorothy."

The Dalziels retrieved Robin and settled in. "I just hope we're out of here tomorrow morning," Dalziel muttered.

"Relax. That's what he told you."

"He has whims that turn into compulsions, especially when he's drinking and bullshitting. A royal ego. But he'll want me to get back with his new toy as fast as possible. That's a blessing."

Precisely at six, they were ushered into a multicarpeted, barn-sized dining hall, Snyder's idea of an English lord's hunting retreat. A pile of logs was snapping and crackling in a fireplace that a person could stand up in. Books in maple shelving covered the walls to shoulder height. Above the books were Snyder's trophies, heads of every possible game animal from every possible place: Siberian tiger, African lion, rhino, ibex, moose, grizzly, wild boar and muskox. Snyder's rifles were ranged upright, military style, on a rack close to the dining table.

In case the roast runs off, Dalziel figured. In case some guest objects to the bullshit.

The other guests were talking quietly with Ida, in a knot near the fire. Snyder himself stood posed not far from the entrance, whisky glass in one hand, the other gripping an elephant tusk that was embedded in a pyramid-shaped block of ebony. The tusk arched far over Snyder's balding head, and Snyder was a tall man.

As they approached him, he brought his glass around and touched it to the tusk. "My latest," he said. "What do you think? Shot him in Kenya. Biggest set of tusks ever recorded, they tell me. Dorothy made a film of that hunt. I know you're both interested in big-game hunting, so we'll watch it after dinner in our theatre."

"What happened to the other one?" asked June.

This was overheard by a young woman in the other group, who laughed and came over to stand beside Snyder, sliding her arm around his waist. She was blonde, dressed in form-fitting pearl-grey slacks and a pink blouse.

"Daddy let the elephant keep it," she said.

"That elephant doesn't need tusks anymore," muttered Snyder. "It went to my Masai guide, as is the custom in Kenya." He turned to the Dalziels. "This is Dorothy," he said. "Our filmmaker."

"I really want to be an actress."

"Crap," said Snyder.

Snyder led them over to the other guests. "Our pilot," he said. "George Dalziel. And his wife, June. Charlie Lavergne, who runs the biggest automotive-supply dealership in eastern Canada, which he's trying to sell to me at an inflated price. He's a wicked card player and a fine shot, as I've discovered on our firing range. His wife, Grace. And Colonel Sandy McNabb and his wife, Betty. Sandy's my hunting buddy. He's president of the American Campfire Club, and a world authority on guns."

Dorothy yawned. Ida excused herself to attend to the kitchen.

"All kinds of guns," said Snyder, winking.

"A hobby," said McNabb.

"Hobby, hell."

McNabb scowled.

"I'm interested in what the papers have been saying about Indian trappers in the Northwest Territories," said Lavergne to Dalziel. "How they can't compete with whites. I can't credit it."

"Indians are better trappers," said Dalziel, "but they don't have to trap. If things get rough, or if they don't feel like it, they can go to the agent and get pogey."

"Talk to Chief Tetso in Fort Simpson," said Snyder. "A first-class trapper and hunter, but he can't keep his own sons out on the line."

"So we're doing too much for them?"

"Absolutely," said Snyder.

"We're doing the wrong things," said Dalziel. "Put in roads, airstrips, wireless stations, schools and hospitals, just like anywhere else. What they don't need is more handouts and special privileges."

"Huzzah!" said Snyder. "Oh-oh. Ida's signalling me. Soup's on."

So saying, he opened his arms wide and herded them to the table.

16

WHILE DALZIEL WAS fetching Snyder's new plane, and Zenchuk was putting in time in Edmonton's bars, Eppler was tramping north along the Nahanni River's right bank, past the end of Joe's part of the trapline. Along the way, he checked a short distance up any tributary creeks. After two days, finding nothing, he crossed, hauling out his hatchet and chopping at the ice ahead as he went. Reaching the other bank, he turned back and made his way past the outlet of the Rabbitkettle River and the giant hotsprings on the opposite bank, again checking up any creeks.

Now he was looking for the camp that Dal had pointed out on the flight in. That camp was as far south as he would go on his hunt for the killer, a dozen miles as the crow flies from their cabin on Rabbitkettle Lake. He needed the food there, especially the rice that Dal had mentioned. All he had left now were a few prunes and some moose parts.

The weather held, overcast but with only a little snow, and

the afternoons were warming up, even though the sun broke through only briefly. Some of the higher south-facing slopes were already bare.

Directly across the river from the hotsprings, he crossed a patch of muskeg that had partially melted. On the moss and log mounds, underneath thin patches of snow, he noticed clusters of cranberries. It was better than finding gold. He ate what seemed like gallons of berries. As he finished, he noticed that a submerged log nearby had been stripped clean of moss and berries. Claw marks were visible on the bark. Beyond the log he saw gigantic footsteps, heading away from him, and some piles of blood-red scat.

"The neighbours are already starting to wake up, Kubla. Something else to watch out for."

Dalziel's camp was identifiable because of the cache, behind an open bluff in a stand of spruce. Eppler could see from his side of the river that the camp was deserted. He crossed, again testing the ice with his hatchet for overflows, then made his way up the riverbank, over the bluff, across a small clearing and into the trees. There he found a couple of full fuel barrels and the cache, neatly covered with a tarp and tied down.

Eppler downed his pack, removed his snowshoes and pushed the ladder, a notched log, from where it leaned against an adjacent tree, over against the cache. He climbed the ladder, holding onto a support tree, untied the tarp and looked underneath. He found a house tent—there would be a log foundation for it somewhere in the clearing—along with three bags of traps and some tools. Beneath these was a bag of rice stuffed into a kerosene tin, a wooden lid wedged into the top of the tin. Also he found a small bag of prunes and a can of lard. No tobacco.

Eppler sighed, and proceeded to carry down the food. He loaded half of the rice into his own bag and took the lard and bag of prunes. The rest of the rice would stay in the cache, in case he got Joe's killer alive and took him south.

He tied the tarp back in place, climbed down and swung the ladder over to its tree. Then he headed to the river, continuing up the right bank toward the hotsprings at the mouth of the Rabbitkettle River. He arrived there an hour later and climbed onto the tufa hills, weaving past open pools of steaming water. It was a strange landscape. He'd heard it described but had to see it to believe it. No wonder the old explorers wove rumours of a tropical valley some-where above the Nahanni falls. The interesting part was that the headhunting Indians were supposed to be led by a beautiful female who liked white men. Or was it a beautiful white female who liked men?

Either way, he'd like to run into *her* right now.

He stopped to examine one of the larger pools. An in-experienced or desperate man might come here expecting refuge from the cold or even just a nice bath. But Eppler had been told that the pools were treacherous, and they looked it. They didn't seem to have bottoms, even the smaller ones. As far down as he could see, there were different-coloured bulges of submerged tufa. Tufa was porous and crumbled easily. If you got too close, and the crust broke, you'd never be able to claw your way out. You'd simmer to death.

Eppler angled down, off the tufa hills, looking for tracks. He crossed the Rabbitkettle again, checking carefully for overflows, and made his way up the riverbank for a couple of miles, then circled through the woods toward the lake. Soon he was standing at the contorted mound of undisturbed snow that had been his cabin.

Murderers were said to be drawn back to the scene of the crime, but not this one.

The trip had cost him over two weeks. His circle, starting and ending here, had covered 60 miles, not counting forays up and down the creeks.

No sign of anyone.

17

THE TRIP TO Fort Erie, the repairs and the flight home took nine days. Dalziel phoned Snyder from the airport.

"It's about time. Let's go."

The group arrived just as the ground crew was gassing up the Fairchild. Jim Ross, Snyder's regular guide, and the young driver emptied the Packard, stuffing everything into the cargo hold. There were deliveries from various stores, some obviously connected more with Snyder's hunting party than with his pitchblende mine. A fair amount of booze went on, for example. Also, a cook turned up.

Dalziel remembered that Snyder seldom went without his apple pie, even when he was hunting.

Ross got Dalziel to one side.

"The guns are in with the mining equipment bound for Eldorado. Mostly they're Snyder's, and there's enough of them to arm a platoon. The heads will come out bagged with ore samples."

"Our customers don't look that happy."

"Price of radium's dropping."

"Good news for the cancer patients. Lavergne seems okay."

"Got a sense of humour, too. He was joking about taking lots of booze in case you left us stranded."

"Ha ha. Would you turn me in if you had to walk out?"

Ross laughed. "You could turn *me* in for taking hunters where we're going."

"Then maybe we should do the world a favour. I'll fly out by myself, you walk out by yourself. Where's the daughter?"

"Staying home, thank God. She's been bad, writing letters to some Yellowknife prospector. Evidently it's all my fault. I was supposed to be watching her."

"What happened?"

"It was last November, and we were heading north to bag a musk-ox for daddy's room. At Yellowknife, she was running around town in her snug fur coat and leggings, blonde hair bouncing, filming everything. The boys were going nuts. While daddy was busy at a meeting, that lunatic McMeekan used his pet raven to tempt her into his sled and out onto the lake with him and a pal. She said it was so she could film the town from out on the ice. Daddy was furious. McMeekan's pal got her address, it seems, and God knows what all else. McMeekan would love to write about that little joke in his stupid newspaper, but he's scared of Snyder."

As soon as they were airborne, Snyder produced a flask and started passing it around. Dalziel refused.

"Against regulations."

"Oh, come on, Dal."

"Dal's got to keep this thing flying, Harry," said McNabb. "And going in the right direction."

"One ain't gonna hurt."

"Lay off. I gotta be back in Washington next week. No time for stupid accidents."

Snyder sulked but was soon asleep, an activity that, Dalziel knew, usually sweetened his disposition. In an hour, they were above the Peace River, heading for the Finlay.

Ross nudged Snyder, who jerked his head up and stared out the window.

"Where the hell are we?"

18

EPPLER WENT FROM the burned cabin back to the Rabbitkettle, toward the outcamp at the halfway point of his part of the trapline.

Returning to the trapline was a lucky decision. Entering the marsh between the lake and the river he saw, on the other side of an open area, a freshly broken willow sapling, almost certainly the work of a moose. He stopped. The temperature was dropping and there was little wind, but it was coming from behind him, angling the lightly falling snow to the southwest. He approached the broken sapling and saw that the branches had been snapped off in the direction of the river. Then he saw the tracks, fresh, well defined, with tufts of snow still falling into them. It was a bull moose for sure, the prints large and well rounded, and it was taking its time, heading southeast.

Eppler hesitated. He needed meat; within a couple of days he'd be hungry, and Kubla hungrier. But there was a killer in the area, who would hear a shot if he was anywhere within two or three miles.

Which he probably wasn't by now.

Eppler decided that there was no choice. He moved off the trail, planning to get ahead of the moose and intercept it from upwind. A few minutes later, he was disappointed to cross the moose's tracks again and see that the prints were now twice as far apart as they'd been before, with long leg furrows embedded in the snow.

Probably got wind of me, he thought. He followed straight on, since the moose was moving away as fast as daylight was fading. He came to the riverbank, saw the tracks cross the river and then, when he scanned the opposite bank, peering though the shoreline willow, saw his quarry. It was motionless, perfectly outlined between two trees. He quickly removed his pack and laid it on the ground. He removed his snowshoes. He stretched out on the snow, using his pack as a gun rest. His 30-30 lever-action Winchester was a touch light for the distance, so he fired at a point slightly above the moose's back. The animal dropped where it was.

As he crossed the river, he could see no movement from the moose. On closer inspection he saw that it was still alive, watching him.

"Okay, okay," he said softly. "You had a few years."

Not like Joe.

He cocked his rifle, aimed it at the neck and fired. The moose jerked once and lay still.

Eppler bled it and started to gut it, throwing the offal to Kubla. But it was too dark.

Better take my time, he thought, make myself comfortable.

He took the hatchet out of Kubla's sidepack and stamped his way upstream to a patch of dry spruce that had caught his eye as he was crossing the river. He dropped four spruce and dragged them back, laying them lengthwise in a pile. Using the moss on the branches he lit a blaze in the middle of the pile, kicking branches off the trees and feeding the fire until it shot up to his height and the trees were blazing steadily. Now a cheering, yellow light extended over his work and he finished gutting the animal, warming his hands as he worked. Then, using hatchet and knife, he quartered the meat. After that, he was too tired to do much else.

He feasted on the heart and kidneys with a half-dozen boiled prunes. He drank an entire billy of tea, then another. This is the life, he thought. But then he remembered Joe.

Eppler rose from the fire and set up his lean-to, using a snowshoe to shovel snow a foot deep against the tarp. He framed both ends with green spruce boughs and piled snow against them. Then he made a bed of the finer boughs and spread another tarp on them. His eiderdown went on that, the canvas folded over on top of it. He adjusted his fire closer to the open side of the lean-to and climbed in.

Two hours later, the cold wakened him. The fire had burned out the centre of his logs and died down. He got up, lifted the ends of the logs together and climbed back into the eiderdown. Usually he performed this routine without really waking up, but on this night he was thoughtful. As he watched, the hot embers fired the logs and the heat of the flames once more reflected off his canvas and seeped through his eiderdown and parka into his back.

He'd hang the meat back in the bush a ways. Make jerky to carry on the next part of his search, and to stash for his trip out. Then north again, but this time on a circle to the west, toward the big mountain that Dalziel, on the flight in, had called The Cathedral. If the killer wasn't there, he was nowhere to be found.

Then he passed again into a deep and dreamless sleep, warmed by the fire that didn't lose its glow until the first rays of the sun peeked over the horizon.

19

ON THEIR WAY back from Edmonton, with a fresh drum of gas in the back, Dalziel and Zenchuk dropped into Fort Smith, where they fuelled up and spent the night. Then they proceeded to Fort Simpson, where they purchased a mountain of sacked groceries. While Dalziel topped up the Robin's tanks, Zenchuk went over to Andy Whittington's, picked up a 26-ounce bottle of rum and told the old man they were taking the dogs.

"I'll miss 'em," said Andy. "They were actually letting me get within 20 feet of the tent before I threw the food."

"You're playing with your life, Andy."

"Never met a dog I didn't like, but I know Dal don't want his dogs spoilt."

"Spoilt nothing. He wants 'em *mean*."

The temperature was near minus 30 with a light east wind blowing and the cloud ceiling high. The two partners unloaded the gas barrel and replaced it with the groceries for Wade and Lomar, and the bundles of pelts. Then they ordered the dogs in. They flew west up the Liard River, a wide highway of ice between rolling, spruce-covered hills. A low mountain ahead indicated the mouth of the South Nahanni and the little settlement of Nahanni Butte. They dropped in to the log buildings of the Eppler-Mulholland trading post to sell their pelts.

"Good to see you boys," said Jack Mulholland. "But I'm surprised. Prices low in Edmonton?"

"No time to take them there," said Dalziel.

Zenchuk heard Daisy Mulholland moving about in her kitchen, and went in search of coffee.

"We heard you flew Mary Littlejohn out for an operation."

"She's doing fine."

Mulholland picked through the bundled pelts and wrote some figures on a sheet of paper. "Comes to $850, Dal."

"You're paying the same price as Northern Traders?"

Mulholland nodded.

"Good," said Dalziel. "Send the cheque to my Edmonton address."

"It'll be in the next mail."

"Anybody coming and going through here?"

"Just some Indian parties on the Liard. Nothing on the Nahanni. I'm wondering how Bill and Joe are doing."

"Worried about your little brother? It's just a hop over from where I drop Nazar. I could do it for $25. If I don't turn up here in a day or two, you can assume everything's okay."

"Can't afford it, and Bill wouldn't like it. He wants to make good money this year. I figure we'll be paying you to fly in after breakup to pick up the pelts. I kind of hope that's what happens, anyway. Daisy's worried as hell about that skinboat idea, but she thinks Bill will see reason in the end."

"I told him they could raft the pelts out. It's a lot of work, but safe enough if they wait for low water. In case they decide to walk, I showed them the route to Faille's."

"Let's hope they walk. By the way, how did it work out with that stove? Did the boys patch one together all right from those empty kerosene tins we threw in the plane?"

"Yes. Whoever built the cabin must've taken the stove when they left. Probably some Indians in a big skinboat. Bill wired the stove together while I showed Joe the line. When we came back, he'd just finished dousing a fire he'd started in the wall. He said a spark jumped out of a crack in the stove and ignited some of the moss chinking. We wired the tins tighter and made tea."

Jack laughed. "I'll bet that scared the hell out of him."

Leaving the post, Dalziel and Zenchuk flew northwest, up the South Nahanni, increasing altitude steadily. Below them, the river was braided at first, one to two miles in width in places, with up to a dozen channels meandering through the forest. Ahead, the land rose rapidly, the vague outlines of tilted plateaus visible in the distance. Soon the braids became one channel. Then the river disappeared, obscured by a canyon. At that point, on the left bank of the river, a puff of steam rose from a small hotspring. The canyon sides were high and straight, so views of the water were only momentary. The plateaus on either side of the canyon were dotted with boulders and patches of scrub birch and spruce. In a few minutes, the slash of the canyon ended in a broad valley, Deadmen Valley, with the big delta of Prairie Creek to the east and another braided river, the Meilleur, coming in from the west. The headless bodies of Frank and Willie McLeod were buried near the Meilleur, close to where they'd been found, in 1907. And later, in a similar position a few miles upstream, the other headless body, which the police believed belonged to the mysterious Weir.

Then a second canyon, this one deeper than the first, with a small valley above it, and then the twisting third canyon, with its hairpin turn near the top. Above the third canyon, the country opened up, smooth eroded ridges and sugarloaf mountains to the northeast, and serried ranks of ice-capped peaks to the northwest, the granite heart of the Mackenzie Mountains where Wade was waiting.

Dalziel swung left over the mouth of a big river that flowed in through flat, thickly forested country from the west. This was the Flat River, the South Nahanni's biggest tributary, favoured by the Indians as a way over the territorial divide into the upper Liard or the great lakes of the Yukon, and frequented by the Fort Simpson trappers and prospectors because of the legends of gold, because the trapping was good and because the South Nahanni was blocked, just above the mouth of the Flat, by whirlpools, white water and, finally, the 300-foot vertical drop of Virginia Falls with its fang of rock splitting the flow.

There was a portage around the falls, along the right bank, but it was several days' work packing supplies and dismantling the wooden river scows and carrying them and the engines to the top. No one trapped or prospected above the falls except Dalziel and Faille, who entered that country on foot from Faille's cabin on the Flat near the mouth of Irvine Creek.

No one really knew much about what either man was doing in there, and both seemed to prefer it that way. Dalziel was making money, for sure, and Faille just liked to wander, using as an excuse his search for the McLeod Mine.

"What are you going to do when you find it, Albert?" people would ask.

"Nothing," he'd say. "Maybe I'd just like to start a gold rush, get a lot of people to come here. They'd say, 'It's the Nahanni Gold Rush. Albert Faille started it.'"

Forty-five minutes later, Dalziel circled down over the mouth of the Caribou River, which flowed into the Flat from the west, and landed on a gravel bar covered in snow and ice. There was a cabin on the edge of the forest, a man standing in its door.

"Good, John's off the line," said Zenchuk, speaking the first words in the couple of hours since they'd left Nahanni Butte.

Lomar was glad to see them and the flour, syrup, straw-berry jam, tea and (especially) rum that they'd brought in. He made up a stack of pancakes and prepared coffee. They ate, then Dalziel chose three dogs and began loading them into the plane.

Zenchuk joined him. "Are you going to top up with gas?"

"No. Each of the tanks is about half full, and I've got to go high to get over to Glacier Lake. I'll use the barrel that I left at Bill and Joe's."

Zenchuk smiled. "So you'll check on them?"

"There's also a couple of barrels at our camp below the hotsprings."

"Maybe I should go with you."

Dalziel shook his head. "I'll meet you in Simpson in June."

"I tell you, Dal, Wade worried me. What if you bloody well *don't* meet me in Simpson?"

"Then you'd bloody well better tell everyone about him."

"Okay. Do it your way. Fly over here on your way to Landing Lake, so I know you're all right. Better get goin'. It'll be late when you get there."

"There'll be a moon."

20

DALZIEL TOOK OFF into a clear sky, heading due west, the Flat to his right and the Caribou to his left, both disappearing behind him. In a few minutes he passed between the round, mile-wide lake that Bill Clark had graciously named after another of his pilot backers, Stan McMillan, and a smaller lake, the source of McLeod Creek. He spotted a column of smoke to his left, near the top of the creek. Gus and Bill were busy mucking out one of their holes.

He'd met them there a couple of years ago, and they were still looking for the lost McLeod Mine. Somewhere along that creek, it was supposed to be. Or on Borden or Bennett creeks a bit farther west. Or maybe, if you listened to Faille, not there at all but on the South Nahanni, above the falls. The legend of the lost mine had inspired numerous minor rushes on McLeod, Bennett and Borden creeks, the last one, only two winters back, involving about 40 trappers. Someone had come into Whittington's bar with a story clipped from the *Edmonton Journal.*

And what a story it was! A map, penned by Willie McLeod himself and left with a priest at Fort Liard, had come into the hands of Wop May, the war ace who'd helped bring down the Red Baron and tracked Albert Johnson, the Mad Trapper, by air. May was a good guy, and it was he who'd convinced Dalziel that he should get a plane and told him how to go about it, but May was also a grade-A bullshitter who wanted more than anything else to be a fixture on the front page. The story then went on to say that May had flown in, located some old sluices, axes, shovels and whatnot, half buried under the first snowfall of the season, and staked the area. After 30 years, the spot had finally been located. But who would stake the actual motherlode?

Over the hills they went by dog team, pots rattling, parkas

flying in the breeze: Eppler, Faille, Turner, Lindberg and their neighbours from up and down the Liard and the Mackenzie. A wonder no one had died. Others flew in—MAS made a small fortune over two weeks. Some hired Indian guides. Diamond'C was there. Chief Charlie. Luckily for some, May and Clark had left Kraus in there to work their claims. Kraus, a most—some might say overly—generous man, was cleaned out of groceries. Most of the trappers had underestimated the country between Fort Simpson and the creeks. A lot of dogs got eaten.

Dalziel remembered it well. He'd been passing through, trapping marten in choice places and moving on, when they'd all turned up. He'd had to lift his traps and leave; there wasn't a moose or caribou anywhere to feed his pack dogs. Kraus and Clark, and Harry Vandaele and Milt Campbell, were the last ones left.

Dalziel's way now was directly up the Flat River to its source farther north, a string of lakes just east of the Yukon Divide. He was there in slightly less than an hour. Then a sharp right to the northeast at the end of a big lake, pinched in the middle, that Nazar thought of as two lakes and had called the Flat Lakes, though he later determined that they weren't the source of the river. Dalziel kept urging the Robin up, following a creek that he'd named after Nazar, a creek that flowed into the bottom end of the Flat Lakes. They had been together when they found the route up this creek and over into the Rabbitkettle River, four years ago, before Dalziel had even thought about flying. They were opening up good marten country and having a bit of fun besides. In the years since they'd teamed up and left Dease Lake and Telegraph Creek, this was the farthest north they'd been, and the best trapping country they'd ever seen.

And there was no sign of anyone, not a single, crazy prospector. Not even Faille, so far as Dalziel knew, had come as far as the headwaters of the Flat River, though, judging by the signs and stories, he was getting closer every year. No one ever knew where Faille would turn up.

Zenchuk Creek came down a valley with round hills to the south and serrated ridges to the north. It featured a precipitous two-step waterfall and, just to the east of the fall, a hospitable spot where they'd shot a moose and built a cache. At the top of the pass there was a small lake, with an island on the north shore. The lake fed into the Rabbitkettle River, which flowed straight east for 60 miles or so, past the lake where Bill and Joe were trapping and into the South Nahanni.

But Dalziel stayed high above that small lake, swinging north over a jagged ridge. Then he dropped over an icefield. Glowing in the light of a half moon, the icefield, with its 11 arms of ice flowing out between cracks in the surrounding ridges, looked like a fat white spider. He followed it down to its main drainage, a creek that shot out from beneath a rugged ladder of blue ice, tumbled through a long granite canyon to some gravel flats and flowed into Glacier Lake.

This was the biggest lake he'd ever found in this country, a good four miles long at least. The north side of the lake was gently sloped and heavily wooded with large spruce, the ideal environment for marten, none better. The south side was steep, with three prominent deltas, but even there the trapping was good. At the outflow of the lake was Wade's cabin, which must have been built by the Indians, maybe a decade ago, unless Faille had come this far up the South Nahanni and into the lake.

Dalziel came down on the snow-covered ice and immediately circled and slid back to the head of the lake, turning right into a small bay on the north shore. This was where he and Zenchuk had stayed when they first laid the trapline around the lake. He was completely hidden there from any point on the rest of the lake.

When he stepped out of the plane, he was relieved to feel a slight breeze blowing up the lake. The dogs jumped out after him, circling and watching him intently. They would earn their keep. Wherever Wade was, they would find him.

He tied on snowshoes, strapped on his pistol in its shoulder harness, hoisted his rifle and led the dogs the short distance across the ice to the shore and into the tall timber. Here the trapline trail began. He started at a half run, along the north shore. The trail had not been used. He stopped near a large tree to check a trap, which was easy to do. Marten were attracted to bright colours, so each spot was marked by a picture of a red tomato, the label off a Royal City brand, tacked to the tree directly behind the trap. June collected the labels for him, steaming them off the tins, getting tins from neighbour ladies, then drying the labels and placing them neatly in a box.

He always thought of her when he saw them.

No trap.

"Son of a bitch," he muttered. "The bastard isn't even working."

If Wade was coming to see what was happening, he'd come up the easier ground on this side of the lake. If he was on the other side, just being tricky, or working that part of the line, if he was working at all, it could be harder to find him. Assuming he had seen the plane, was still around, was alive.

Just what I need right now, Dalziel thought, resuming his steady run down the lake. Another corpse for Truesdell.

21

EPPLER HAD BROKEN camp on the Rabbitkettle that morning. He'd left carrying 20 pounds of jerky, another 20 packed in Kubla's bags. The toboggan held assorted frozen cuts of meat and chunks of fat. The rest was bagged and hung in the branches of a tall spruce, waiting for him when he headed out, either south to Simpson with the killer or, if no killer, west, up the Rabbitkettle River, over the Yukon Divide and into the Alaska Panhandle somewhere, probably Wrangell.

And then? He wasn't sure. He'd always wanted to see Australia.

If he headed out. If someone didn't kill him.

He'd crossed the Rabbitkettle and angled through the marsh, over to the South Nahanni. Then, weaving in and out of the fringe of bush along the riverbank, he'd moved north, staying off Joe's section of the trapline in order to look for signs along the river.

Nothing. Now he was settled at the mouth of the small

creek where he had camped before, on his first circle. He kept to the bush and made an almost smokeless fire out of some dead willow branches. It was early to be settling in. He could have put in a couple of hours beating his way up the creek, but good camping spots would be rare and he still felt lazy after three days processing the moose. Also, although the wind was light, it was from the east. Not good for heading west in pursuit of a killer, but maybe it would change overnight.

The temperature was dropping again. Winter's last gasp, and probably his, too. It was the third week in April. The mid-afternoon sun had, over the past few weeks, brought the snow cover down by almost half, to about two feet. Water now accumulated in the centre of the South Nahanni, then froze at night. Early that afternoon, the sun had produced real heat, and he'd felt it warming his shoulders through his parka. Finally he'd stopped to push back his hood and pull on his beret.

That's how it would be in Australia, he thought, all the time. After more than a decade in the far north, a man could stand a bit of heat.

Tomorrow it would be up toward the big mountain. It was a long shot, but there was nowhere else to search.

22

WADE HAD BEEN dozing when the distant sound of an engine intruded on his dreams. He ran out of the cabin just in time to see the plane, a black smudge on the moonlit snow, turning out of sight·at the far end of the lake.

It was Dalziel, Wade was pretty sure. The visit was expected, but why had he pulled in up there? Had he been to the other lake, seen the burned cabin? Were the police with him? If so, they would die with the pilot, and he'd be long gone before anyone figured it out.

Wade ran back into the cabin to collect his rifle, pistol and ammunition. As he fumbled the ammunition into the small pack he carried on his patrols, he remembered that there was an old slide about a third of the way along the lake's north shore, a jumble of trees, rocks and mud that must have come down with the snow a few years ago. The slide had almost reached the shore, leaving a narrow passage between it and the water. He could get up behind the corner of the slide with a view to the lake, which was bright enough to show anyone passing down it or close to the shore.

He moved quickly, never appearing on the lake, gained the slide and found a spot that gave him a clear sightline through two large rocks and some tumbled trees. He removed his snowshoes, stashed them behind him in the fallen trees and settled in.

He'd done this sort of thing many times since he'd headed into the bush. The trick was to stay put, not move. The only way the pilot would know he was there was if he could smell him.

Dogs! When he had first encountered the pilot and his partner in their camp, there had been dogs all around him, snapping at his pants and snarling. Would he fly dogs in here? Not if he was just coming for the pelts. But if he was coming for the pelts, what was he doing at the other end of the lake?

He cursed himself. He'd have to move to be sure, to a spot up higher, get flat out on a rock between some trees, with some space around him. The pilot couldn't be close yet.

He lurched to his feet and turned toward his snow-shoes, but there was a sudden explosion of movement from around the rock to his left. He couldn't see them! He got one shot off at a speeding shadow and heard a yelp, but others were instantly on him as he floundered in the deep snow, teeth penetrating his leggings and his arm, twisting, dragging him down.

Then a voice said, "Stop moving or they'll kill you."

He stopped. The dogs still held his leg and arm in an ago-nizing grip.

"Let go of the rifle."

He let go, and the rifle was taken from his hand. "Get them off me!" he cried.

"Why? You just killed one of them. You laying for me too?"

No answer.

"How come you're not working the line?"

"Wasn't gettin' nothin'! I was gonna move the line down the creek."

"Funny," said the pilot. "Marten tracks everywhere. There won't be anything along the creek. I thought you said you knew how to trap."

"I got pelts!"

"Where?"

"In the cache."

"We'll just look at those pelts, then. Easy."

The dogs let go of him, but backed off only a few inches. Wade sat up. He could see Dalziel's shadowy form squatting below him, two rifles, one of them his, slung over his shoulder. Wade had a sudden impulse to lunge, try to get at the pilot and then worry about the dogs. But Dalziel seemed to guess his thoughts; he lifted his arm and pointed a big pistol straight at his face.

"Take your pack off."

Wade removed his pack. Dalziel dragged it to himself with his free hand, not taking his eyes off Wade. He shoved his hand under the lid.

"You expecting the German army?"

Wade didn't answer.

"Get up, put your hands out and lean on that rock."

Wade obeyed, struggled up, and was promptly relieved of his pistol and hunting knife.

"Where's that .22 you brought in?"

Wade hesitated. He could lie, saying he lost it down the hole when he was getting water.

"Just make it easy and tell me. If I can't find it, I'll have to hog-tie you until morning."

"In the overhang behind the cabin."

Dalziel shouldered Wade's ammunition pack and stepped aside, indicating that he wanted Wade to precede him and move toward the cabin.

"Don't know if I can walk. Your dogs tore me bad."

"Take all the time you need. I've got a feeling I already wasted lots of it anyway, bringing you in here."

Wade did take his time, exaggerating his limp though it hurt enough. He thought of stalling by pretending he couldn't walk any farther, but where would that get him? His right pant leg was damp with blood. Dogs! If he stalled, the pilot would set them to guard him and go on to the cabin and the cache himself. The best bet was to pretend that everything was normal.

"Got worried there was someone around," Wade said. "Heard a shot when I was down the creek a few weeks back."

No response.

When they came near the cabin, Dalziel said, "Wait here" and, to the dogs, "Stand."

"How about me waiting in the cabin? I believe I got frost in one hand."

"Rub it then. Just don't try to walk or they'll bring you down again."

Dalziel passed in front of the cabin and vanished around behind it. Then the door banged open, a light flashed and the window glowed a steady yellow.

The dogs stood unmoving, nosed into his legs, eyes on his face, teeth bared.

The light in the window disappeared suddenly but re-appeared in the trees beside the cabin. It moved up to the cache. A minute later, it descended from the trees and returned to the cabin. The window glowed once more.

Then the pilot was beside him, the .22 on his shoulder.

"You can go into the cabin now. Easy."

"I got some tea on the stove."

"I'll camp up the lake and bring the plane down early in the morning. Get ready to go out to Simpson."

"Why?" Wade almost sobbed it out. There was an RCMP post there, and a magistrate.

"You've been here over five months. You've got two or three months' worth of pelts, and the season's almost over. It'll be a waste of money coming back to get you."

"I'll walk out myself. You don't have to take me out."

"Don't be crazy. Pack up your stuff and be ready in the morning." The pilot turned abruptly, ordered his dogs to heel and headed up the lake. Wade watched him vanish almost instantly, as if he'd walked right into the colossal silhouette of Cathedral Mountain.

Wade limped to the cabin. Inside, he checked his leg. It was punctured in six places, torn badly just above the back of the knee and swelling fast. He tore up a clean shirt and wrapped the wound. He fished the tobacco and lighter from under his bed and rolled a smoke, making a mess of it. But smoking calmed him.

He'd load up everything he had for the trail and head down to the canyon where he'd stored the dead man's rifle. He'd rest there a couple of hours, until dawn, then keep going.

23

AT 5:00 A.M., Dalziel crawled out of the pup tent he'd strung between some trees on the small delta near the plane.

A whistle brought his dogs loping up to him. He turned, rummaged in the tent, extracted his pistol in its shoulder holster and buckled it on. Then, after strapping on his snowshoes, he untied the tent and bundled it up with its contents, packing it out of the bush and over to the Robin.

The kerosene space heaters he'd set up before going to bed were both still working. He removed the engine bonnet, turned off the heaters, set his controls and pulled on the prop. After the third pull, he looked up. Here and there in the brightening sky, a star. On the fourth pull, the engine kicked in, as expected, blowing a puff of blue smoke and filling the valley with its roar.

He glided down the lake, letting the dogs run along beside him.

Wade's couple of months of trapping were done well, udging by the bundles in the cache. He must've gotten bushed, pulled the line in and hunkered into the cabin. That would explain yesterday's ambush.

Whatever the poor bugger's problem was, Dalziel would load his pelts, truss him up like a turkey and fly him out, stopping at his camp below the hotsprings for fuel. That was the best way, open and above board. Get him away from Bill and Joe and settle with him at Fort Simpson.

Let Newton and Truesdell figure it all out, if they were curious. Let them earn their government cheques.

He found the cabin door open, the bed, table and stove stripped, tracks heading toward the creek. He sighed and went back to the plane, removed the bolts from Wade's rifles and pocketed them, shouldered his own rifle and struck out along Wade's trail, the dogs ahead. After a half-hour, he left the trail and made a circle around the cabin, seeing no sign that Wade had doubled back. The stupid bugger was running. Or he was just hiding somewhere down the creek, waiting for the plane to leave.

Dalziel decided to fix it so Wade couldn't stick around, and then clear Bill and Joe out of their place. He'd tell them about Wade getting bushed and trying to ambush him. That, and a free flight out with their pelts, should convince them that it was time to leave.

Back at the cabin, he climbed up into the cache and took out the kerosene tin. He removed a haunch of moose. Better the dogs have it than Wade. He decided to leave the furs for the time being. The plane would be heavy enough once he picked up Bill and Joe with their equipment, dogs and pelts. In fact, some of their stuff would probably have to stay behind. He could get it, and Wade's hides, when he came through after breakup.

He loaded the moose into the plane, then soaked the inside of the cabin, making especially sure to get the kerosene into the spaces between the logs. He used a piece of firewood to smash in the one tiny window, crumpled some paper, dumped Wade's pile of bark, moss and kindling on it, soaked that with kerosene and lit it. He left the door open.

By the time he'd lifted up off the lake, turned and flown over the cabin, flames were shooting out the door and window.

24

EPPLER'S TRIP UP the creek soon degenerated into a thrash. After a couple of hours he saw a small lake, and approached it carefully. Afraid of being seen, he did not step out on the ice, though he was sorely tempted since the surface snow was drifted smooth and hard. He started to struggle his way through the bush around the lake.

Suddenly he heard an airplane, a distant drone. Through the trees, he spotted it momentarily. Dalziel, almost certainly, and he was dropping into Rabbitkettle Lake maybe, or his camp near the hotsprings.

The sound faded.

Kubla gave a low bark.

"Pretty strange, eh boy? What does it mean? Should we carry on through this jungle or go back?"

Kubla heaved forward and stopped, a front foot lifted. Eppler knelt beside him and cocked his rifle. "Stay," he whispered.

Something was moving along the shore of the lake, not more than a hundred feet away. Eppler stared, trying to focus on the image flickering through the trees. A pack with a sleeping bag strapped on top. A hooded head.

Which suddenly turned toward him.

"Stick your hands up, mister," shouted Eppler.

But a rifle was instantly lifted and fired, wide of the mark, blasting wood off a tree a few feet away. And in the time that Eppler blinked, the figure was crouched and floundering off the lake toward the trees. Eppler stood and fired through the trees at a shoulder. The figure lurched but kept going. Kubla bolted, but Eppler grabbed at his saddlebag and was pulled onto his knees.

"Hold it, boy. No runnin' up the bore of that maniac's rifle. I got a feeling I'm gonna need you."

Eppler held Kubla's collar and eased forward. He could hear crashing ahead, and he soon intersected a snowshoe trail coming up from the lake and heading into the bush.

"He's running for cover, but unless he's stupid he's not going to let you get downwind, Kubla. He's goin' back where he came from, and he'll keep goin' so long as this breeze holds."

Eppler examined the tracks. "That's our boy, isn't it? Same repairs on his snowshoes. So he was up here all the time. We gotta go around him and get downwind."

Then he noticed blood.

"We winged him. Good! He'll have to see to that. C'mon."

Eppler crossed the killer's trail and headed straight through the bush, parallel to the lakeshore, hoping to get downwind. Kubla followed.

But Wade, clutching his coat tightly around the burning wound on his arm, had no intention of letting the dog get around him. He circled through the bush and intercepted his own track just before it hit the lake. He was on a broken trail now, and he ran.

Eppler arrived at the point where the tracks met.

"He's fast, Kubla. Guess we didn't hurt him all that bad. Look, though. He's still droppin' blood. All right. We missed our chance to get around him right now, and we can't run up his trail without getting blasted, so we'll zigzag on after him. That's okay. We want him alive, so what we'll do is try to wear him down, take the fight out of him. He can't shake us in the snow."

Eppler turned and went back to where he'd left the toboggan. He dragged it down to a spot near the lake, tramped down the snow, lit a fire and made tea.

He was strangely happy. "We found the bugger," he said to Kubla. "We hurt him a bit. Now we'll play him around as if he's game and make him pay for Joe."

25

AS DALZIEL CUT the throttle and drifted toward the South Nahanni, he opened the door and flung Wade's pistol and two rifles out, followed by the bolts and the knife. No one would ever find them in that bush. He turned above the South Nahanni, followed it down and then circled over the mouth of the Rabbitkettle into Rabbitkettle Lake. He saw, before his skis hit the lake, that the cabin was gone.

Damn!

The fuel was gone too. And the trees around the clearing were burned black.

It looked like a war zone. He pulled close to the cabin, tied up, left the engine on idle and let his dogs out. Plowing up the trail to a hummock of glittering snow that sat where the cabin had been, he noted that the pathway had been used not too long ago, before the last snowfall, maybe. He stood and stared at the mound of snow, realizing by the shape of it that the walls of the cabin had been blown out.

But the door frame, with the door still attached, was in an odd position against the charred wall, not burned. He shoved it upright, brushed off a skiff of snow and saw a bullet hole in the frame, just below the top hinge. Dalziel examined one side of the frame and then the other. The bullet had come from outside and emerged inside the cabin.

He pushed the frame back against the wall, walked to the cache, set the ladder against it and climbed up. The tarp was well secured. He untied it and pushed it back.

Eppler's can of paint. No rifles. No pelts, either.

They're up at Glacier Lake, he thought. They're the ones in Wade's cache. Wade must've done it, just like he'd most probably killed Czybek.

Dalziel felt a chill run up his spine. Wade would have taken any rifles, too. There were no extra rifles in his cabin or cache, but he could have stashed them somewhere. "Might've been damned lucky I slept through the night and woke up this morning," he murmured.

It would take days to find Wade now. Weeks, if he was smart enough, fearing the dogs, to just clear out. Too much time.

I should've told them about Wade, Dalziel thought again.

Then he shook himself out of his reverie, and the noise of the plane washed back into his ears. He looked to see his dogs nosing around the trail by the cabin. He covered the cache, descended, pushed the ladder onto an adjacent tree and returned to the Robin.

In a few minutes he was in the air again, his fuel gauge close to zero. Another 20 or 30 miles left, maybe. He flew over the hotsprings, the rising sun making rainbows in the columns of steam. Then he drifted down onto the South Nahanni and pulled into a little cove. Above the cove hung the bluff on which he'd put his camp.

The camp looked untouched, maybe a smudge of an old snowshoe track going up the riverbank and over the bluff. The barrels were there, thank God. Otherwise, he'd have had to cut down a few trees, winch the Robin far up into the bush behind the camp, drain the oil and walk out.

After fuelling, while the dogs chewed on Wade's moose, Dalziel checked the cache. The rice tin was lighter—only a few pounds left, he noticed when he opened the lid. Any other food he'd cached here was gone.

With luck it was Bill and Joe, heading for Irvine Creek.

He took off downriver. About 20 minutes later he swerved to the right, over the rolling hills, saw Irvine Creek below and banked to the left, following the creek down to the Flat River, keeping low in the valley, looking for signs of a snowshoe trail, of anyone moving.

No one. He circled the cone mountain at the mouth of Irvine Creek, flapped his wings over Faille's cabin, flew down the Flat and circled Zenchuk's, flapping his wings again. Then he headed upstream.

A half-hour later, he dropped into Landing Lake, which was tucked into thick forest just above and across the Flat River from the outflow of Borden Creek.

WADE STOPPED IN the canyon alcove where he'd
stashed the rifle he'd taken from the man he'd killed, and
attended to the wound on his arm, using part of the dressing
he'd put on his leg. The smaller tears on his leg were swollen
and purple but drying. The bigger ones opened as soon as he
unwrapped them. The graze on his arm was deep enough to
cause heavy bleeding; though he'd held it together, his shirt
sleeve was soaked with blood.

He shoved a couple of prunes into his mouth and left,
planning to take the moose in the cache by his cabin and
make for the alpine meadows due north of Glacier Lake. It
was a long way, and he'd be out of food in a week unless
he found game, but higher up there would be bare ground
on the south-facing slopes; his tracks wouldn't be so easy to
follow. He'd move on in a big circle to the South Nahanni,
build a raft and get on the river, where he could quickly gain
some distance. Along the way to the river, at any place where
they'd have to come to him from upwind, with no easy way
around, he could try an ambush. The spot where he would
leave the Nahanni would be untraceable.

An hour later, Kubla led Eppler into Wade's camp in the
canyon alcove. Eppler quickly took in the lean-to frame, the
fire ring and some shreds of blood-soaked cloth, then followed the track back out of the canyon.

When Wade broke out of the forest near Glacier Lake,
he saw wisps of smoke hanging over the water. Then he saw
where they came from. The cabin was burned down to two

rounds and still hot. He hadn't left much there in his rush to pack up and get away from Dalziel, but it had included a few small packages of food. In the cache, no moose. The pilot meant him to move on.

He should've taken the time to put the moose into his pack.

Wade went around to his blinds, collecting a hatchet, a jackknife and a few more shells. Then he headed up the north shore of the lake, stopping only to cut the hind legs off the pilot's dead dog. These he stuffed into his parka pocket to thaw.

Eppler arrived at the cabin just as Wade reached the upper end of the lake and started his ascent of the creek that ran in from the north. Staying in the willow, Eppler carefully examined the smouldering cabin and the surrounding area. Plumes of smoke were still rising and drifting lazily up the lake. Nothing else was moving, so he headed north, planning to intersect the shore of the lake about a mile up.

"Look at that lake, Kubla. Never would have guessed anything that big was up here."

An hour later he arrived back at the lakeshore and intersected the track of the repaired snowshoes, heading for the top of the lake. The killer was walking on a track made by different shoes, coming down the lake. Eppler turned back to the cabin, noting on the way that this was another of Dalziel's traplines, the trees marked with labels.

"The bugger has a line even here," Eppler murmured.

Then he found signs of a struggle around the base of an old slide, blood on the snow and a dead dog with its hind legs missing.

"Our man's hungry. That's good."

Continuing down the lake, he noted ski tracks out on the ice. Dal's plane had come down to the cabin, then made a turn and headed back up the lake.

In the cache, he found his and Joe's pelts.

Eppler lit a fire close to the cabin, made tea and grilled some meat. As he and Kubla settled in for the night, he said, "I still don't get it, but this looks like an eviction. Some guy who didn't work out. Maybe Dal was even flying down to tell us about him. Better late than never, I suppose, but too late for Joe."

27

AT LANDING LAKE, Dalziel drained the oil from the plane and stored the buckets carefully in his cache. He removed the skis, putting on the pontoons. Then he set up his tent. The next day, he laid out traps in the most promising section of the line, around the south end of the lake.

While he worked, he couldn't stop thinking about what might have happened up at the lakes. It had to have been Wade who had blown up the cabin. Probably he'd killed Bill and Joe. Why else would he run off rather than fly out?

If Wade had no rifle, he wouldn't live long enough to get out. There'd been next to no food in the cabin, and only the moose in the cache, and all that was gone now. Even if he'd had Bill's and Joe's rifles stashed somewhere, he had no dogs to carry his stuff. He was as far from anyone as you could get, and he didn't know the country. A man could go for weeks without stumbling on a moose. Caribou were more dependable and less careful, but didn't provide enough fat. If Wade was heading for the South Nahanni, it was a dangerous route, offering the temptation to walk the ice and avoid the jungle along the shore and the climbs around bluffs and canyons. The Rabbitkettle River would offer the same temptation, if Wade figured to cut back up it into the Yukon. It would take a month, moving steadily, to go out the way they'd flown in. Either way, the rivers would be especially dangerous and would soon be breaking up and uncrossable. If Wade survived long enough to put out on the South Nahanni— assuming he could manage to put a tight raft together—he'd be dead in a day. A single man couldn't handle a raft on the Nahanni, especially during runoff.

As for Joe and Bill, if it was they who'd gone into the cache at his camp below the Rabbitkettle hotsprings, that had probably happened before the explosion, since there was no sign of anyone going down Irvine Creek. He'd advised them to check there if they ran out of food.

By his second evening, Dalziel was glad to chase these thoughts out of his mind with a book. He kept books everywhere, a habit that amused Zenchuk, who read little, was indeed impatient with books, but who could play cards—even solitaire—non-stop for days, or sit and toss a knife into the wall for hours, or simply stare into space.

At Landing Lake, Dalziel had stashed Byron's *Don Juan*, his favourite from Grade 10 for its restless hero who went ceaselessly from one country, friend, lover or situation to the next, always discovering disappointment but satisfying curiosity, cynical but finding hope in constant change.

As he read, he had an idea. He'd say he put Bill and Joe at Glacier, not Rabbitkettle Lake, and he wouldn't even mention Wade. If the police checked the cabin at Rabbitkettle Lake, they'd see that the place had been blown up, and he'd have some serious explaining to do. He'd have to admit that he'd dropped a killer in to work his line. A real Mad Trapper. Truesdell and the *Edmonton Journal* would have a field day with that. He and June and Nazar would have to go into hiding. At Glacier Lake, there'd been only a cabin fire—it happened all the time—and the boys had headed out, leaving their pelts in the cache. Probably they'd tried to walk out. More likely they'd tried the skinboat idea. Either way they'd run into trouble.

What I have to do, Dalziel thought, is clean out the traps Bill and Joe set on the line at Rabbitkettle, and get rid of that door frame.

28

WADE WAITED IN ambush near the top of the creek, hiding in a blind he'd built there months back. He'd determined then that the creek was the only way out of the upper end of Glacier Lake, which was boxed in by glaciers to the south and granite cirques to the west. At the top of the creek there was a barren, ice-streaked alpine. To the north a pass, saddled with a glacier on one side and a low bluff on the other, led over to country that drained into the South Nahanni.

He spent most of the night in the blind, until the moon set. He dozed despite himself and woke up shivering, realizing that his pursuer would have had no trouble sneaking up on him. In the morning he stripped and gnawed on one of the dog's legs, sucking any fat and chewing on the stringy, metallic-tasting meat. At noon, he moved on, cursing.

They were letting him get tired.

Three hours later, Kubla led Eppler over to the creek and the spot where Wade had sat out the night.

"Look at that, Kubla. The guy's got hunting blinds set up all over the country! In strange places, though. No moose would be crazy enough to come through here."

Not far from the blind, Kubla found pieces of bone and shredded skin.

"Some lunch."

29

THAT NIGHT DALZIEL heard wolves howling at the far end of the lake. He had a good idea what they were up to—stripping his traps. In the morning he set out some bait, the remains of a moose he'd put in his cache over a month earlier. He placed the bait just off the big island near the lake's far end, and hid himself as comfortably as possible in a tangle of spruce on the island's shore. They appeared at dusk, six of them, moving warily from the mainland out onto the ice. When they were at the moose, he fired, getting them all. Two had damaged pelts—he'd plugged them through the guts. The other four were head shots, and he skinned them right there.

A mistake. In camp the next morning, just as he was scraping the wolf pelts, pulling them over a large log that he'd elevated on a crossbrace and rounded with a sharp axe, the dogs set up a ruckus, and within minutes he had visitors that he might have expected.

Gus Kraus and Bill Clark were teamed up with Harry Vandaele and Milt Campbell, and they were heading out, down to Faille's. They'd crossed the Flat just below Landing Lake.

"One hell of a crossing," Kraus explained as the other three stood by. "Thick ice on our side, over the deep channel. We walked to the edge of the ice, and saw that it was shallower, so we crossed there. The water was slow but chest deep. Ho-leee!"

"I'm done for life," said Vandaele. "Castrated. Probably they'll fall off tonight."

"No loss for a prospector," said Campbell.

"Did you notice any ice farther down?" Dalziel asked, trying to sound welcoming.

"No, and we walked down quite a ways looking for a crossing. But I'd guess there's ice not too far down. We could be stopped for a few days, but we have to build a couple of rafts anyway. The fact is, Dal, we heard you fly in here, and we could use some grub. It's been a bad year for hunting. Just before we left, Harry and Milt set about 20 snares and ended up with only four bloody rabbits! That settled it. We've got a bit of old jerky, but nothing else. Harry and Milt are clean out too. If you've got some food to spare, we can pay with gold."

He held up his prospector's vial, showing off some coarse gold and a couple of nuggets.

"How much flour gold?" Dalziel asked, examining the nuggets closely.

"Only about a pound. There's a small mountain of dirt left to be sluiced yet, but no sign there's much in it."

"I've got no tobacco, but I've got extra tea and rice, a few pounds of flour, some oatmeal and a small bag of prunes. Enough to get you down to Faille's, at least. It's all yours. And you can take some meat out of the cache for your dinner tonight."

"How much, Dal?"

"You don't have to pay. You boys have given me plenty of business."

Under other circumstances, he might have charged, cost price at least, but he liked Kraus, a friendly if talkative man. And he was trying to ingratiate himself with Clark, who was eyeing the wolf pelts.

"Can we use your camp tonight?" Kraus asked.

"Of course. Help yourself to any firewood or equipment you might need. Don't bother asking."

"Nice pelts," said Clark.

"They cleaned out the back part of my line a couple of days ago, and made the mistake of coming back for more. I just can't bring myself to waste the pelts."

"Don't blame you," said Kraus. "Beautiful, aren't they? Good for keeping warm at night. I guess you've got to keep them here, eh? Or get them south where you can sell them legal."

Clark said nothing. Probably, Dalziel thought, Truesdell would be hearing about the wolves in a couple of weeks. And this time there were four witnesses, though Kraus would be a reluctant one, and the others too.

Now it wouldn't be safe to fly the wolf pelts out. Too bad. Kraus knew his stuff; in Edmonton, they were worth as much as marten.

"Crazy," said Vandaele, running his hand over the pelts. "These are beautiful! You can kill them but you can't skin them?"

"You're not supposed to kill them," Clark explained. "The law is for the local Indians. They don't like killing wolves. They won't handle the pelts. Bad medicine. If they know you have them, they stay away from you. But it's impossible to stop white trappers from killing them, so the Territorial Council had to settle for slowing the killing down by making it illegal to trade in wolf pelts."

"Most places pay a bounty on wolves."

"There's never been a bounty here."

"This place is run for the Indians," said Kraus. "The officials and the Hudson's Bay Company—they'd like all of us out of here."

"Not the prospectors," said Clark. "We don't compete."

Damn right, thought Dalziel. The Indians already know there's no gold here. If there ever was any, they took it out decades ago.

Four lean-tos went up, around a cooking fire. Kraus came to get the food.

"I'm turning all the flour into bannock, Dal," he said. "Any leftovers, we'll eat on the way out. Come and get some biscuits while they're hot."

30

BUT DALZIEL WORKED late that evening, finishing his wolf pelts, taking advantage of a half moon that rose in a clear sky just after the sun set, keeping a bright fire going and working close to it.

Only much later, when the four were sitting around the fire, poking at it with sticks and talking sleepily, did Dalziel bring a half-full bottle of rum and his tin cup over to the fire.

They all poured themselves tea, and Dalziel added a liberal shot of rum to each cup.

"Here's to a safe trip out," he said, raising his cup.

They drank to that.

"Harry and Milt are gonna guide us down," said Kraus. "This is a first for me and Bill. We've always flown out with Wop."

Vandaele sipped his drink and moaned ecstatically. "That's so good," he said. "Good food. Good company. A good drink. I can only think of one thing I want more."

"Better company?" Campbell suggested.

Everyone laughed.

"Gold, you fools!" Vandaele shouted, grinning maniacally.

"They say it can't buy love, but how do I know for sure if I've never tried it? God, how I'd like to try."

"You sound like a character in a Robert Service poem," said Dalziel.

"A favourite of mine and especially Milt's," said Vandaele. "Hit it, Milt."

"He's the man from Eldorado, and he's only starting in
"To cultivate a thousand-dollar jag.
"His poke is full of gold-dust, and his heart is full of sin,
"And he's dancing with a girl called Muckluck Mag."

"And what were you quoting at me, Milt? Just two or three weeks ago?"

"Gold! We leapt from our gas pumps. Gold! We sprang from
our stools.
"Gold! We wheeled in the furrow, fired with the faith of fools."

"Gas pumps. That's a good one, Milt," said Vandaele. Dalziel cut in:

"Partner with partner wrangled, each one claiming his due;
"Wrangled and halved their outfits, sawing their boats in
two."

Vandaele laughed gleefully. Dalziel reached out with his bottle. Clark refused a second shot of rum.

Vandaele feigned shock.

"When do you go out, Dal?" asked Campbell.

"You boys will be in Simpson before me. Lake ice takes longer to thaw. Normally I'd hang around for the spring beaver hunt, but the ban's on this year."

"Down south they trap them all winter," said Vandaele.

"Not really worth it in this country, unless there's nothing else to go for. The ice is too thick. You have to wait until there's some open water and they start swimming around. It's easy to shoot them from shore, and then use a pole to snag them and drag them in."

"Doesn't that bugger up the pelts?"

"I use a .22 Hornet and aim for the head, so there's just a small hole that doesn't hurt the pelt."

"How much will you take out of here, Dal?" asked Vandaele.

"I did well in the early winter, before I flew out. Right now I'm just here to wait for breakup, but I'll get a few marten before I leave, if I can keep the wolves off my line."

"Will you pick up Zenchuk and Lomar on the way down?" Kraus asked.

"No. They have the scow."

"Think we can hitch a ride with them?"

Dalziel nodded. "There'll be plenty of room in the scow. Nazar and I already flew most of our catch out, so Faille's the only one with a full load, and he can move all of it, with his dogs and equipment, in his freighter canoe. There's a possibility that Bill Eppler and Joe Mulholland could show up at Faille's for a ride out, but if they do they won't have their pelts with them."

Clark looked puzzled. "Jack Mulholland told me they were coming down the Nahanni on a skinboat."

"I suggested a raft," said Dalziel. "So long as they can wait for low water. But if they can't, I told them to head down to Faille's on foot."

"I bloody well hope they do!" said Kraus. "What would put an idea like a skinboat into Eppler's head? I got a good impression of him when he came through a couple of winters ago, during the pseudo gold rush. He borrowed a bucket of lard from me, and he was careful to return it the next summer when he came up with Dick Turner and Albert Faille to work their claims. He guessed I'd need it, and I did."

"They might as well shoot themselves as float down the Nahanni in a skinboat," said Campbell. "You need something that can take a beating from big waves, and a few brushes with rocks and logs."

"Dal, we saw you fly up the river," said Clark. "Did you check in on Bill and Joe at Rabbitkettle Lake?"

"They're at Glacier Lake," said Dalziel, launching his story.

"Never heard of any Glacier Lake."

"It's a little ways farther north. I've got a line there too."

"Jack told me they were at Rabbitkettle."

"They changed their minds on the way in," said Dalziel. "But no, I didn't go that way. I went over to my old camp on the Coal River to get some things."

"It's a whole new world," Clark continued, shaking his head. "I can't even imagine it. Trips that took weeks, even months, are done in hours."

"You don't like it?" Dalziel asked.

"No," said Clark. "I have to say I don't. Old-fashioned, I guess. The next generation won't know how to live in the bush."

"And we don't know how to throw spears," said Dalziel.

Kraus laughed. "That's it, Dal. Bill and I use planes all the time for our work, and we're bloody glad to do it. Of course we get a deal, since Leigh Brintnell at Mackenzie Air is our main backer, and Wop May's put in some of his own cash too."

"But you're not flying now?"

"We figured to save some money. The fact is, the shine's wearing off our little enterprise. Brintnell's in for another year, and then he's pulling out, right, Bill?"

Clark shrugged. "I'm going to have a talk with him."

"I wouldn't think Leigh Brintnell had enough spare change to go prospecting," said Dalziel.

"He don't," Kraus guffawed. "I worked at the airstrip at Fort McMurray before I came here, so I know the talk. But Harry Snyder's the money man behind Mackenzie Air. He and Leigh are close. Without Snyder, MAS wouldn't exist. Leigh's a hell of a good flier, but money don't stick to him."

"Snyder's a great believer in the lost McLeod Mine," said Clark.

Vandaele sighed. "So were we. That's what got us here. Two years and a few dollars in the past, eh, Milt?"

"A few lost dollars saved from a few lost years working the gas pumps," said Campbell, shaking his head. "Some family wondering what the hell got into us and a couple of girls quickly forgetting our handsome faces."

"Dozens of girls, Milt. Hundreds even."

"I hate to say it," said Clark, "but I'm partly responsible for spreading that story, though I sure didn't mean to. All I was doing was advertising for backers, mostly in Edmonton and Calgary. I got Wop interested, and then he helped me spread the word."

"It was Wop told me," said Kraus, "and that's when Bill got a partner."

Clark laughed. "Every trapper around Simpson and Nahanni Butte, and a few from even farther off, left their traps in the bush and came tearing in. You remember, Dal. You were here at the time."

"I remember."

There was a long pause, Clark sneaking a glance at Dalziel, Dalziel focussing on the rim of his cup.

"That's when Eppler borrowed the fat off me," said Kraus. "They were all clean out of grub by the time they got to McMillan Lake and found our camp."

"Buffoons," said Dalziel.

Only Vandaele laughed. "That's a word I haven't heard since school," he said. "And it pretty well sums up what I feel like right now. 'Fired with the faith of fools!' How many times can a guy get suckered in?"

"Adapt or die, boys," said Dalziel. He held out his bottle and sloshed more rum into three eagerly extended cups, Clark once again abstaining. "There's gold all over this country. Fur is gold. This country's rich with fur, and marten was selling at $40 a pelt a couple of weeks ago in Edmonton. Beaver pelts earn $30. You have to get away from the Liard and the Mackenzie, though. Too crowded."

"Forty dollars a pelt!" said Vandaele. Then, after a meditative sip, he added, "Dal, I've heard you hire men to work your lines."

"Got any experience?"

"I know the country now, and I've been up and down the river a few times. I trapped gophers and coyotes when I was a kid."

"Where?"

"Spruce View. Near Calgary."

"Where'll you be this summer?"

"Milt and I are going to meet up with Fred Turner and my brother Joe and do some sluicing along the Liard with a force pump."

"I'll see you sometime in the summer, then. If you're not pumping up buckets of gold, maybe we can make a deal. My camp on the South Nahanni below the Rabbitkettle hotsprings has been sitting idle this winter. You could go there."

31

THIRTY MILES DOWN the Flat River, Faille was expecting visitors—and they were more than welcome. Last summer, he'd heard that Kraus and Clark were planning on going out by boat or raft, to save money. Their operation on Bennett Creek wasn't producing as they'd hoped, and backers were pulling out. And Zenchuk had mentioned that he and Lomar would make their way up the Flat as soon as trapping was over, to wait for breakup.

"It seems that Lomar doesn't like to play cards," was the explanation.

Faille was sitting in his cabin, feet up on a block of firewood placed in front of his cook stove. He was content. The winter's trapping had been good; there was about $3,000 worth of pelts in the cache. Enough to get the outboard motor fixed. Enough for materials for a new scow. Enough for another winter's supplies, something for Marian and a bit for the bank in Simpson.

A single lantern burned in the cabin, throwing a soft glow. On the stove sat a pot of simmering beans, laced with molasses.

"Going over to the Caribou River a spell," he said aloud to himself. "In the morning. Follow up that third fork. Stay out for a night or two. Maybe get a moose and make the dogs happy. Leave a note and some beans for the boys in case they come early. They'll wait for Albert, the river rat."

He thought for a moment, then stood up, stretched all 5 feet 4 inches of his thick-set frame, turned up the kerosene lamp on his table and stared down at a photo album that was sitting open, a head-and-shoulders picture of a pretty woman with round spectacles and a pug nose. The spectacles made her look quizzical.

"Panned a couple nuggets out of that creek," Faille said to the woman in the photo. "Remember them? Mailed them to you last year. How come you don't write now that I got a permanent address? Still mad at me, I bet." He brushed the back of his index finger along her cheek, blew the light out and turned toward his bunk.

"Couldn't live in town after the war, Marian. Couldn't even live at the edge of town."

Then he heard a shot from downriver. It would be Zenchuk. Outside, the dogs began to howl.

Chuckling, shaking his head, he went to the door and opened it to moonlight. The yard in front of the cabin sparkled with frost. Five huskies bounded across the clearing toward him. He stepped outside and lifted his rifle from where it sat on two pegs driven into the logs just beside the door, under the overhang. He reached into his pants pocket and pulled out a shell, slid it into the chamber and closed the bolt, pointed the rifle to the sky and fired.

He returned the rifle to its pegs and then took a chain off a hook. "C'mon, boys. I'll put you out back. Don't want you tearing into Nazar's dogs."

He returned in a few minutes, entered the cabin, took a railroader's hurricane lantern off its nail on the wall, lit it and then went out again, carrying the lantern to his cache.

"Saved some coffee for just this occasion. Nazar will like that. Better find that pemmican ball, too. Probably they're hungry."

When he returned to the cabin, he left the lantern sitting on a stump in front. An hour later, as he was sitting at his table turning for the umpteenth time the yellowed and ragged pages of an old *Maclean's*, the exotic smell of coffee pervading the cabin, the dogs began a ruckus and the door swung open.

"Good God, Albert. I smelled that coffee two miles down the river. Poor John here is run ragged from trying to keep up to me."

"You're worse than a bear, Nazar, when it comes to coffee."

Zenchuk stepped in and behind him, Lomar.

"Hi, Albert," said Lomar. "The dogs are tied to a tree along your trail to the river."

"That's fine, John. Come on in. Drop your stuff on the bunks. You boys should be hungry."

"We are," said Zenchuk, as he and Lomar peeled off their packs and outer clothing. "We were hoping to run into a moose on the way, but we didn't see a track even."

"They've been avoiding the area, I swear. They've posted warnings."

Zenchuk lifted the lid on the bean pot.

"Those are still hard as nails," said Faille. "But I've got some pemmican."

"We can wait for the beans, Albert," said Zenchuk. "Don't trouble yourself. I'm no lover of pemmican. Hope you don't mind if I just pour myself a cup of this."

"Go ahead," said Faille. "You too, John. But Nazar, you just taste my pemmican before you decide." Faille rose, taking the fist-sized lump of pemmican off his table. "Move that pot over a bit, John, and put the skillet on. Nazar, I'll need your help outside. This is still frozen solid."

Zenchuk followed Faille from the cabin to the chopping block. Faille handed him the lantern and picked up the axe. A sharp blow with the top of the axehead shattered the pemmican ball into a dozen pieces, which Faille and Zenchuk proceeded to pick up and carry to the cabin.

All the while Faille kept talking, enlightening Zenchuk as to the ingredients and virtues of pemmican and which lady in Fort Simpson made the best.

They dropped the pemmican into the frying pan. Once it was sizzling, Faille added one handful of raisins and one of oatmeal. He cooked it until the raisins and oatmeal were soft, the oatmeal soaking up the fat. Then he dished it into three bowls.

"Not bad," said Zenchuk, chewing on his first mouthful. "The oatmeal gives it body, and the raisins cut the fat and sweeten it."

"And the fat makes us strong," said Faille. "Go without fat for too long in this country, and the sky gets grayer, the bush darker, the wolves better organized. I buy pemmican off the Indians every chance I get. This'll carry us until tomorrow, and then the beans'll be ready. After that, we've got to make a serious attempt to get a moose. We got to walk right up to Mr. Moose, introduce ourselves and invite him to dinner."

"We got 50 pounds of flour in our cache," said Lomar.

Faille nodded. "It shouldn't be long before we can get at it. What's the Caribou River look like now?"

"Quite a sight," said Zenchuk. "Thawed from top to bottom, by the looks of it. Shooting right out over the ice on the Flat and flooding the bush. Ice blocks and broken trees everywhere."

After they'd eaten, they poured themselves more coffee.

"Did you know that Eppler and Mulholland could meet up with us here or at the mouth of the Flat?" asked Zenchuk.

"They're down on the Liard. I saw them setting up in their usual spot near the Butte on my way here."

"They didn't bring much in through November and December. I guess that line is pretty well trapped out. Dal dropped in at the Butte in January and talked them into trying up at Rabbitkettle Lake."

"A good idea! They'll do well there. The Liard's too crowded, no doubt about it. So they're rafting their stuff out as far as the Flat and then hooking up with us?"

"That's the trouble. Dal couldn't pin Bill down. His original plan was to build a skinboat and get out with all the pelts straight down the Nahanni."

"A skinboat! Utter suicide," said Faille.

"Dal suggested they use a raft or just leave the pelts in the cache for him to pick up, and walk down Irvine Creek to here. Bill didn't commit."

"Dal's right," said Faille, "but Bill's like a mule when he gets an idea in his head."

Lomar yelped. His pipe had fallen out of his mouth, hit his lap and spilled.

"Better sleep," he muttered.

"There's more coffee," said Faille.

"Gotta sleep." Lomar banged his pipe out on the stove top, lurched over to the bunks and climbed into the top one, not even bothering with his eiderdown.

"Sweet dreams," said Zenchuk.

No answer.

"Tell me, Albert, was Eppler already at Fort Simpson when you came into the country?"

"I don't think so. I think he was still trapping in the Barrens. I believe he had a trading post in that direction, too, at Providence. I met him in '29. He came to Simpson not long after I did, and trapped along the Liard before he partnered up with Jack Mulholland to start the post at the Butte."

"It's a good post. They know what people around here need."

"I'll say. Like the biggest kickers money can buy. There's one out there under my scow that I bought off Jack and Bill last summer. Mind you, I broke it right away on some rocks when Bill and Dick Turner came upriver and sweet-talked me into going to their claims on McLeod Creek. Just had to show those boys how to get a boat through the canyon. Do you think John would mind if I helped myself to another bowl of fine cut?"

"I'll ask him. John, Albert wants to know if he can help himself to more of your fine cut."

No response.

"Silence means consent, Albert."

Faille took the can from the floor and stuffed his pipe, lighting it from the stove and puffing hard until a huge cloud of fragrant smoke once again enveloped his head.

"Do you know the whole story about that murder charge in the U.S?" asked Zenchuk.

"Eppler was an orphan," Faille said. "It's something he and I have in common. He was raised in an orphanage in Winnipeg, but he left there when he was 11 years old and he was on his own after that. Like me, he turned into a wanderer. Both of us rode the rails for a time, hung out with the hoboes. When he was about 18, he was passing through the States, thinking that California would be the place to find work. He arrived in some midwest town, riding the freights, and ate a meal at the café there. The owner was a Greek, and he figured since Bill was a stranger and not much more than a kid, he could get away with charging him a little extra. Bill up and argued."

"As he would," said Zenchuk.

Faille nodded. "It came near to a fist fight except the other customers intervened. Bill threw down what he figured he owed and headed for the tracks, meaning to bed down and wait for the next freight. On the way, he stopped to watch some kids playing baseball. One of them hit a fly ball that went into the grass not far from Bill. The kids couldn't find the ball and accused Bill of picking it up. He said no and invited them to search him and his bag, which they did. No ball. A few minutes later, one of them found it in the grass and the game went on with Bill still watching."

Faille sucked hard on his pipe. Once again his head disappeared in a cloud.

"A half-hour later the police turned up, grabbed Bill and took him to jail. Turns out the Greek had just been shot to death out back of his café and some of the customers that the police talked to remembered Bill and the fight. Bill was in jail for two weeks waiting for his trial. He told me it was the worst time of his life. He got claustrophobic, afraid there'd be a fire at night and he wouldn't be able to get out. A few days into his stay there, a guy in the next cell was taken out and hung, yelling that he was innocent.

"They gave Bill a lawyer, and he contacted the orphanage in Winnipeg. They sent a good character reference. Then the lawyer rounded up the boys who'd been playing baseball, and some customers who did think Bill was overcharged. The kids were the key.

"At the trial, the police admitted that they had no weapon, and the prosecution assumed that Bill had ditched it somewhere. The boys testified that there was no gun on Bill when they'd searched him and his pack, and the way the times lined up, it was clear that Bill couldn't have gone anywhere but from the café to the baseball diamond. So he got off. He says he hightailed it for the Canadian border as fast as he could go, and he didn't stop running until he hit Great Bear Lake. He figures they'd have hung him if it hadn't been for the sheer accident of stopping to watch the baseball game and being searched by the boys. He swore he'd never allow anyone to drag him into jail again."

Faille sucked reflectively on his pipe. Zenchuk poured himself more coffee.

"Poker?" asked Zenchuk.

"Thought you'd never ask."

3 2

WADE TRIED ANOTHER ambush on the barren alpine slope higher up, in a narrow litter of talus at the base of the pass. He laid his track up to the top of the pass, to and behind a strange configuration that turned out to be two long-dead bull caribou who'd got locked together during the rut. Then he went backwards in his track into the talus. From between a couple of boulders, he had a clear view across a snowbowl that was fringed on the opposite side by willow, and could see where his tracks came out of the bush. To his right was a glacier ringing a small mountain; to his left, a steep, rocky slope that would provide cover but make for difficult walking.

In moonlight, the enemy would be visible.

He waited through the afternoon and the night, restless, dozing for too long sometimes, his arm and leg throbbing. Then he waited through the morning.

He was just starting to think that maybe the enemy had given up and turned back when he saw some movement in the willow. The movement stopped, and a few minutes later a column of smoke drifted up.

Christ, he was having his lunch! Wade realized that the smoke was drifting slowly back the way he'd come, and that the dog could be catching his scent.

Lunch lasted all day. Wade lit a fire himself, made tea and then more tea, following it up with the last of his prunes. He was incredibly thirsty. Then he slept, confident that his pursuer would not chance crossing the open snowfield. At dusk, figuring that the dog had caught his scent for sure, he broke from cover.

Eppler, sitting in the willow at the edge of the snowfield, caught a glimpse of him disappearing over the pass.

"We'll cross the snowfield now, Kubla, and make ourselves comfortable in the talus. You keep those big ears of yours open and that nose up."

33

WHEN THE PROSPECTORS got up the following morning, they found that Dalziel was already out on his line.

"A hard worker," said Kraus as he tossed tea into a large pot of boiling water. "Knows what he wants and how to get it."

"Why does he have to break the law, then?" asked Clark.

"What do you mean?"

Clark nodded at the stretched wolf pelts.

"Aw, for God's sake, Bill. You're not gonna worry about that, are you? He'll just use 'em here to keep warm at night."

"Are you kidding? I know Dal. He's planning on selling them in Edmonton. And the law's the law, Gus. If you break it a few times and get away with it, you keep on breaking it."

Kraus shook his head. "Puttin' the law on him makes it hard for us to deal with him when we need him, like now. That's his Orange Pekoe you're about to sip, and his prunes going into your porridge to keep your hair and teeth from falling out, Bill. The scow we'll be begging a ride out on is his, or half his. You want to drive him out of the country, or have him snub us when we need him?"

Clark scooped some tea with his cup and left the fire, to wander through Dal's camp.

"Bill's got his knickers in a knot," Kraus explained quietly to Vandaele and Campbell, who were watching Clark in surprise. "He's a stickler for doing the right thing, but he's pushing it too far this time."

"It sure seems like it," said Vandaele. "If Dal flies the pelts out, the Indians aren't even gonna know. Why doesn't Bill like Dal?"

"Because of something that happened that winter we were talking about last night," Kraus said as he stirred the porridge. "After Bill and me got partnered, we set up on McMillan Lake, put a tent there and a cache. Then we built two more caches, one on McLeod Creek where I was and one to the south on a little lake that drains into the Caribou River. Bill had big plans, you see, that he sold to our backers.

"Later on we found the last two caches had been cleaned out. All the food was gone from the McLeod cache, and Bill's boxes of mineral samples, which were at the cache on the lake, were scattered all over hell's half acre, useless. A note at the McLeod cache, from Dalziel, said Chief Charlie and his group were hungry so he showed them the food. No explanation of the samples. A bloody mess, I tell you, and Bill was mad.

"Finally we ran into Dal and confronted him. No fun, you know. He can be scary, with his dogs milling around, growling and snapping at our legs, and that bloody big pistol hanging over his shoulder."

"I've noticed that," said Vandaele. "What the hell is it?"

"A .38 in a .45 frame. He's good with it, too. Wop told me that a couple of years ago, Dal won a flight to Edmonton off him, in a shooting contest up in Fort Norman. Dal told us that he was here first and didn't want any prospectors around chasing off the marten and the moose and messing up his traplines."

"I can see his point," said Vandaele.

"You bet. Anyway, the next night, after thinking it over, I guess, he turned up at our camp and apologized and gave us back some of our food and also handed over some marten pelts to pay us for what Chief Charlie took. Those pelts paid for most of our winter food! It was a lesson to me. I was happy. But a few days later, Leigh Brintnell flew in some supplies for us and Bill sent out a written complaint to the RCMP with him."

A couple of hours later the four men were scrambling down out of the bush and onto the Flat River, happy to see that the ice shelf they'd crossed before was gone.

Kraus sent Vandaele and Campbell to fall some dry spruce that were clumped together just up the river, trim them and cut them into eight-foot lengths. They floated them down and rolled them onto the gravel bar. Kraus and Clark cut some green poplar, then found firewood and lit a fire to cook lunch. Over tea, Kraus described his plan for the rafts.

"Looks like we'll have to build two rafts. Water's too shallow for a big one. Here's the technique. There'll be four of those spruce logs to a raft. The green wood is for crossbraces to hold them together. When the dead wood expands in the water, the raft gets good and tight."

He scraped some rocks to one side, picked up a stick and sketched the raft in the sand. The four spruce logs had two notched poplar crossbraces on top, two below, bound tight with snare wire.

"Here's what the notches in the poplar look like. Got it?"
Vandaele and Campbell nodded.

"We put a light platform in the middle," said Kraus, "to

hold the stuff out of the water. Tie the rifles down separate and loose, one piece of rope from the raft to the trigger guard, just long enough so you can kneel, load and fire if you see any game. Stuff them under the cover. Same with the swede saws for sweepers."

"No paddles?" asked Campbell.

"No, they're a bugger to carve. Poles will do. We'll never be too far from shore."

"Cold wet feet for a while," said Clark.

"It's worth it," said Campbell. "We could be in town in four or five days if we're lucky with the ice. But I think we're going to miss our comfortable scow and kicker, eh Harry?"

"Yeah. But there's a portage about halfway to Faille's, and we won't miss packing the scow and kicker over that. How long was that portage, Milt? I never noticed because my back was killing me. It seemed like eternity."

"It's a good mile. We'll have to build two more rafts when we get back on the river, unless there's ice."

They all sat silent, watching the fire. Then Vandaele said, "Tell me the truth, Gus. Would you work for Dalziel? If you were me?"

"Sure. With him, you'd learn a lot. He's the best stick man I've ever met. Even Bill would admit that."

"That'll all end when Truesdell shuts him down," said Clark. "Which he will."

Kraus shook his head. "You gotta hand it to Dal, though," he said, tapping his finger on his forehead. "It's a great concept. He can lay out all the lines he wants. The law puts no limits on that, so long as you're not intruding on somebody else's line. He can plant guys on the lines and watch the money roll in." With that, Kraus stood up and looked at Clark. "I ain't saying I'm going to work for him, Bill. I know how to trap. But in a year, I can get my trapping licence, and after that there'll be a trapline where I'm prospecting. *If* I'm prospecting."

"C'mon, Gus," said Clark softly. "There's gold where we're looking. I'm sure of it."

"Maybe. But look at Faille. He does his prospecting when he can afford the time. But when he can't he traps and makes a good living. He's prospected up and down the Flat and along the Nahanni above the falls. Never found a damn thing, but what've *we* found? He's got a good cabin in Simpson, some scows and motors, and three or four solid cabins along the Flat and up the Nahanni. That's what I call a life. That's what I call getting somewhere."

"Which is what we'd better do right now," said Vandaele.

"Yeah," said Clark, rising. "Let's put those rafts together."

34

EPPLER STUCK TO Wade's track over the pass. He could see the clumsily backtracked trail, the killer's attempt at a trap, with the latest trail on top of it. The man was tired and not thinking right. No one would waltz across a snow-field toward a pile of boulders! Anyway, Kubla had known exactly where the killer was.

The triple tracks ended at a couple of caribou skeletons with antlers locked. Now a single track moved down a smooth slope where the pass narrowed into a valley with what looked like a canyon starting at the far end. In a few weeks the canyon would hold a raging creek, but at this time of year it would still be smooth walking. It would also be a likely spot for the killer to be waiting again in ambush, if he had the energy. Pretty soon now, he'd give all that up and just start to run.

Eppler reached the head of the canyon and pulled in among some rocks. It was late afternoon, with an hour of light left, but he didn't want to get too close to the killer or be in the canyon at night. He chewed some jerky, watching Kubla nose his share around on the snow, trying to soften it. Then he crawled into his bag and dozed, sitting up, his rifle propped nearby and Kubla stretched out beside him.

35

BEFORE THEY REACHED the portage, Kraus, Clark, Vandaele and Campbell ran into an ice bridge, a good 50 yards long, arched clear across the water, and they pulled into shore to think the situation through. They could see under the bridge to the other side, and there was enough clearance, but no one had the stomach to try floating through. The bridge could collapse suddenly. Or one of the rafts could snag on the side of the ice, lift up, block the flow and get pushed under.

"You try it, Harry."

"I'm sure you'd be more successful than me, Milt."

So they unloaded the rafts onto the riverbank, carried all the stuff around to the other side of the ice bridge and then decided to try kicking the rafts loose and snagging them at the other end with a long pole.

It worked. They reloaded and continued for another mile, only to find their way blocked by a small mountain of ice slabs, the river gushing around it, tearing at the bank and flowing on top of the ice.

"Damn it," said Kraus. "We're not getting anywhere now. I say we start walking."

"I think the portage trail is just ahead," said Vandaele.

It was a boring trek, pushing through endless birch and willow and wading the ice-cold streams that flowed into the Flat. But at dusk they had luck: Kraus saw a cow moose and yearling calf on the other side of the river. He knelt and plugged them both. Then he crossed the ice with Vandaele and Campbell, cleaned the moose and cut them up, packing the quarters back. Clark set up camp. They ate moose-meat steaks, medium rare, with the last of Dalziel's prunes and some bannock. Then they hung the rest of the meat.

"Tomorrow," said Kraus, "we'll pack what we can down to Faille's and come back for what's left, depending on how needy Faille is."

36

BY NOON, THE canyon opened into a broad, forested valley. Eppler could see, far below, that the river running through that valley had wide gravel flats on both sides and only a moderate drop. Probably it drained into the South Nahanni.

The killer's destination, Eppler thought. There'd been no tricky stuff in the canyon—the track went straight down the centre and out the other end. And if his objective was to get to the Nahanni, there could be only one possible reason—to put out on a raft and make his escape.

But that had to be three or four days off.

Eppler started a circle north of the tracks, and camped in deep forest that night, not lighting a fire.

Less than a mile south, Wade too was spending the night in thick bush. He hadn't made it onto the more hospitable gravel flats of the small river because he kept tripping on willow and birch and crashing, exhausted, to the ground. During the night, he would sleep for short periods, then awaken in the midst of frightful dreams of soldiers shouting, dogs barking, coming closer. The dogs would come through dense bush to seize him and tear at him; he had no chance to bring his rifle around to shoot them.

Once, the roar of a rifle woke him. In amazement he found himself on his knees, up to his chest in the snow, darkness all around, his rifle shouldered. He'd fired at some figures appearing at the edge of a shell crater in which he'd taken refuge.

The shot, echoing up the valley, awakened Eppler. He sat up and looked at Kubla. "What's he trying to do, boy? Shoot game in the dark? Keep us up all night so we're too tired to chase him? He's not far away, is he?"

Wade crawled back into his bag. Later, Alf and Marty appeared, with news of a German detail coming their way across no man's land. But he could see they were already dead, their uniforms torn and bloody, their faces chalky, their eyes all white. He watched them fade into smoke, beckoning him to follow.

37

KRAUS, CLARK, CAMPBELL and Vandaele arrived at Faille's at noon. They got a warm welcome, especially when the reception party noticed the moose they were carrying. Men and dogs consumed everything that the four prospectors brought in.

"We'll go get the rest of the moose this afternoon," said Kraus as they finished eating. They were sitting contentedly around Faille's outdoor fire spot, each on a block of wood, sipping tea. Faille built the fire up high.

"Did you know that Bill and Joe could show up here for a ride out?" Clark asked Faille.

"Nazar was telling me. I can't quite figure what they've got in mind, but I guess we're not expected to wait around."

"According to Dal they were on Glacier Lake, not Rabbitkettle like they planned," said Clark.

Zenchuk blinked, realizing that something must have happened with Wade. "They must've changed their minds on the way in," he said. "Don't blame them, either. That's probably the best marten country I've ever seen."

"I didn't know Dal worked that far north," said Faille.

"He went even farther north," said Zenchuk, "trapping live marten for breeding. He got the marten all right, but Truesdell got him."

"Was Dal charged?" asked Clark.

"Nope. The law's vague or something, and Dal had cleared it with Newton. When we got back from Edmonton they handed Dal a hundred-dollar fine."

"Which he paid out of his pocket change," said Clark.

"Do anything special in Edmonton?" asked Kraus.

"We flew Mary Littlejohn there. She had appendicitis and Truesdell wanted her to have it out in a regular hospital."

"She okay?"

"Had it out, last I heard, and recovering nicely. What's that noise, Albert?"

Faille leapt up. "The river! Let's have a look!"

They walked the trail, a quarter-mile through an old burn that had grown in thick with head-high birch and willow. The crashing became nearly unbearable, and the men covered their ears with their hands.

At the river, they saw that flood water from higher up, carrying loose chunks of ice, was flowing over the surface ice, to within a foot of the top of the bank. The force of the water, like a giant hand, was sliding pieces of loose ice along the ice below, lifting some as they jammed against others, flipping them over, welling up around them and forcing them on. The far bank had collapsed, and trees were angled over the ice, their tops bobbing and twirling. As the men watched, a tree tore loose, fell onto the ice and was instantly caught and chewed up by the shifting chunks.

"We should be able to leave tomorrow," Faille shouted over the din. "Usually she goes out right from here to the Nahanni in a day."

"I'm off for the meat," said Campbell when they got back to the cabin.

"Me too," said Faille. "Gotta move. Is two enough?"

"I'll go," said Vandaele.

Kraus intervened. "You work on the raft, Harry."

By the time Vandaele, Zenchuk, Lomar and Clark, armed with Faille's tools and a roll of snare wire, walked back to the river, the water was down three feet below the bank and hurrying out with a sullen muttering and the clunking of coffin-sized pieces of ice.

They built the raft right at the riverbank, where it could easily be pried over the edge and slid in. As they worked, they took time for coffee, cigarettes and talk. They finished at dusk and returned to the cabin. Later, a distant shot indicated the approach of Faille, Kraus and Campbell. Vandaele fired an answering shot.

"Just a few miles up," said Faille as he broke into the clearing, approached the fire and dropped his pack, "the river's ice-free clear to the bottom. In the morning, we're on our way!" Kraus and Campbell were close behind him.

After dinner, Lomar, Clark, Campbell and Kraus crawled

into the bunks in the cabin. Faille, Zenchuk and Vandaele wanted to keep talking, and decided to sleep outside around the fire. Vandaele had already made himself especially comfortable, sitting on a folded Hudson's Bay blanket and leaning back on a plank that rested on one of Faille's stump seats. Regularly he'd stand and turn or hold his plank close to the fire to heat it or sit with his back to the fire, flexing his muscles and moaning contentedly.

"I'm surprised to see you and Milt," said Faille, looking at Vandaele and pulling his pipe out of his pocket. It was already loaded, and he lit it with a piece of dried twig he'd found nearby on the ground and poked into the fire. "Thought you were heading home as usual when you dropped in on me last October, and wouldn't be back until summer."

"That was the plan. But we had some luck on our way out. Milt sold a couple of our claims to a Vancouver publisher who happened to be in Whittington's bar checking up on the McLeod bullshit. Naturally Andy was feeding it to him by the shovelful. The $200 got us a flight out, with the publisher and his buddies, to Yellowknife, and we cadged plenty of free drinks and a lot of attention from a group of Consolidated mine managers who also wanted to know about McLeod Creek. To put the old tin lid on it, we got taken in by our own stories. Our claims started to look very promising. After a week of high society, we took our sore heads across the lake to Waterways and got the train south in time to hug our mothers and take part in the neighbourhood moose hunts. We played cards through December, opened our Christmas presents and then jumped a boxcar in the Calder Yard. We worked our way from Dawson Creek to Fort Nelson as assistants to a teamster on a freight sleigh. Dal found us there and brought us in after New Year's. Since then, reality has reasserted itself. Oh yes. We've hit bedrock and sluiced everything we dug up, using meltwater. No luck, and that's the end of it. It's over for us, Albert. Now we've got trapping in mind."

"Did you talk to Dal?" asked Zenchuk.

"I did. He suggested his line on the Nahanni just below the Rabbitkettle hotsprings. Do you know it, Nazar?"

"I helped Dal set it up. It's a fine trapline, Harry. Just one thing. Dal's a busy man, and he's only one step ahead of Truesdell. The good doctor would love to ground him forever, so be prepared to take care of yourself. Have a plan to get out on your own."

"From there, you'd have to walk out if you were alone," said Faille. "With a partner, you could use a raft, especially if you waited for low water."

38

EPPLER AND WADE emerged from the forest and stepped out onto the riverbank at the same time, still about a mile apart. Both noted that the river was breaking up. It was a small river, but the main channel, across the ice-and-snow-covered gravel bars, was a six-foot-wide slash of bouncing white water. Uncrossable already.

Eppler, glad to be out of the forest, found a place among

some large boulders and made tea. Wade stayed off the beach and carefully examined the wide gravel bars, looking for tracks. With luck, his pursuer had passed him. But he saw no tracks. Then something moved from behind a rock outcropping just downstream.

Got him, he thought.

But it was the antlers of a grazing bull caribou. When the caribou stepped out into the open, Wade shot it, not even thinking of his pursuer, then slit its throat and scooped blood greedily into his mouth. He scraped some ice off the ground and let it melt down his throat. Right away, he could feel the life coming back into him.

Then he cut pieces to put in his pockets and pack, and moved down the river, gnawing and chewing.

Eppler heard the shot. He put his billy away and shouldered his pack.

"Must've found himself something to eat, Kubla, unless he took another shot at a shadow. We'll see if we can take his lunch away from him. He sure ain't far down."

He stayed in the forest along the edge of the water. Eventually he would see where the killer came out onto the riverbank, but he saw the caribou first, steaming, by an outcropping. Then he saw the tracks disappearing down the river.

"He had a piece of luck. Hope it was his last."

Eppler sliced into the caribou, tossing piece after piece to Kubla. He lit a fire, cut out some ribs and cooked them lightly, sucking greedily on the fat.

39

THAT MORNING, WHEN Faille's guests took their coffees over to the Flat, there was nothing but a few chunks of ice bobbing past.

"Looks darned peaceful after yesterday, don't it?" said Faille.

The men lifted Faille's 18-foot freighter canoe from its winter resting place where it lay flipped over on blocks, the dead engine, paddles, poles and gas cans stored beneath.

"We could wait a day or two," said Kraus. "I've been on rivers before, but nothing like the Nahanni from what I've heard."

"Let's go as far as the Nahanni, anyway," said Clark. "We can check for Bill and Joe, just in case they floated down that far."

Zenchuk agreed. "I hate to think that the rest of the boys are drinking beer, comparing nuggets and telling lies at Whittington's while we're up here chewing on moose."

Faille's canoe held his dogs, pelts, engine, gas cans and personal outfit, with room for at least one other man and his gear. There was little freeboard, so he put Clark, the lightest of them all, in the stern. The raft carried everyone else, with all their gear and Zenchuk's dogs.

The five men on the raft each had a pole. Their feet were in the water most of the time, the raft dipping and wallowing when they moved to pole away from the riverbanks and large rocks.

By noon they were 30 miles away, pulling up to the right

at Zenchuk's camp, just above the boiling but ice-free out-flow of the Caribou River. They unloaded the raft, glad to see the last of it, and dragged Zenchuk's 30-foot scow to the river. While it was being loaded, Zenchuk put the outboard in place and started it, but shut it off once it was running smoothly. He figured on using it only in emergencies, his gas supply being down to what little was in the tank. Kraus turned some of Zenchuk's 50 pounds of flour into biscuits.

Then they were on their way again. By mid-afternoon they were at the mouth of the Flat. The South Nahanni, they could see up ahead, was carrying large slabs of ice, but with lots of open water between. The shore ice, however, was still solid, so getting off the river was going to be difficult.

Pulling into the south bank of the Flat, well back from the swifter current of the Nahanni, they clambered onshore to check for Mulholland and Eppler. There was no sign of recent occupancy around Faille's old cabin, but not far away, on a gravel bench farther off the river, they saw fresh cuttings and the signs of a campfire.

"These weren't here when we came through last September," said Zenchuk.

"We camped up there," Lomar agreed, pointing.

Back at the boats, Faille asked, "Do you want to do a few more miles?"

"There's still some hours of light," said Clark. "Let's keep going."

"What about that shore ice?" asked Kraus.

Clark frowned, then said, "How about if you guys give Albert and me a few minutes to get ahead. If you see us heading off the river, follow our example. Albert can look out for any trouble and find the best way to shore."

"We have to find eddies behind points of rock, or log piles at the head of gravel bars," said Faille. "They'll get us into calm water. Any creeks coming in will be ice-free, and that's our best chance to get off."

The others wanted to keep going, so Faille and Clark pushed the canoe out into the current. As soon as they swung south into the South Nahanni, Vandaele, Campbell, Kraus, Zenchuk and Lomar followed in the scow.

"Harry, you got good eyesight for distances," said Campbell. "You keep your eye on Albert."

Plying his paddle to help keep the scow straight in the water, Vandaele fixed his eyes on the distant figure of Faille, who regularly stood up to gaze downriver. How the hell does he do that? Vandaele wondered. They were making at least 20 miles per hour, and the current was forcefully jerking and bouncing the scow around. The canoe would be even less stable.

By dusk, it seemed their gamble was paying off; they were through the Third and Second canyons and out into Deadmen Valley, just above the Meilleur River. Faille intended to put in there and check First Canyon from the cliffs the following morning. He and Clark were working their paddles hard, trying to get closer to shore. Suddenly there was a dam ahead, a solid wall of blue ice and piled blocks that extended clear across the river. Standing up, Faille saw to his horror a whirlpool, a hundred feet in diameter, between him and the ice wall. Kneeling again, he stroked frantically,

Clark following his example, trying to skirt the whirlpool, hoping to pick up enough speed to spin out of it. They flew around once, paddles flailing the water, but dropped in three feet.

Behind them, Vandaele saw Faille and Clark turn a full circle and drop so that only the tops of their heads were visible.

"Pull for shore!" he shouted.

Zenchuk fiddled with the outboard and started yanking on the rope while the rest dug frantically with their paddles. Just as they reached the edge of the whirlpool, the centre of the ice dam broke with a thundering crack, and the pool burped up. Faille and Clark suddenly appeared again, now behind Zenchuk's scow and facing upstream. The scow shot through the widening gap in the ice dam, Zenchuk still jerking on the rope.

With a series of explosions, the ice from the dam broke off, slabs 20 and 30 feet across and two feet thick above the water wallowing madly and crashing into one another. But the Meilleur River delta, up ahead, was clear. They aimed for it, Faille and Clark slowly pulling ahead. When they broke out of the ice and drove their bows up on a gravel bank, Faille and Vandaele jumped out of the canoe and scow respectively, holding the bow ropes. Then, with Vandaele and Faille pulling, and the others pushing off the shore and paddling, they worked their way up into the Meilleur River to a quiet beach protected by an eddy.

Vandaele tied the scow to a willow bush and went screaming into the trees, jumping and cartwheeling. The rest staggered onto land and stood or sat down on scattered boulders, stunned silent. They needed no discussion about staying. Not a word was said. They'd survived because of luck and luck only.

40

THE FRESH CARIBOU meat, and the gradual widening of the river valley he was following, enlivened Wade, gave him hope. I'm getting close, he thought, and I'll go right out onto the big river. I'll use the snowshoes and some pack straps to hold the raft together, lay flat out on it and use my arms to steer. I shouldn't have to go too far before I can get back to shore.

He walked almost non-stop, though his leg wounds slowed him, making him limp, and his arm ached. He figured his pursuer was far behind, still taking his time, hoping to wear him down. Now that tactic would work against him.

The small river made a sweeping turn to the right and he saw ahead of him what had to be the broad valley of the Nahanni, but as he struggled along it seemed to get no closer. Again and again he encountered bluffs, the river churning around their bases so that he was forced to climb up and over. He spent two nights on the bluffs, sleeping in an upright position, rifle in hand.

Eppler followed, hugging the edge of the forest, glimpsing Wade from time to time out on the riverbank, closing the distance.

41

VANDAELE AWAKENED EARLY, took his .22 and walked down the brush-covered banks of the South Nahanni. He flushed some green-winged ducks and swung his rifle around, but they were moving too fast. Then he inspected the bushes nearby and found two nests. He collected a half-dozen eggs, wrapped them carefully in his bandana and started back to camp. On the way, he heard a shot from up the Meilleur River and reckoned it would be Kraus, looking for meat.

Near camp, Vandaele met up with Campbell and Faille, who were heading up the Meilleur to see what the shooting was all about.

"Breakfast omelette," Vandaele said to them, holding up his egg-laden bandana. "Sleep well?"

"Not me," said Faille. "Kept waking up in a cold sweat. I swear that was as close as I've ever come. If that pool hadn't coughed up when it did, we'd have all gone under. I figure the dam was there because First Canyon is jammed with ice. It could still be in there. After breakfast, we'll pull in just below Prairie Creek and go up on the cliffs for a view."

When Kraus, Campbell and Faille returned, they were packing the best part of a two-year-old moose. Lomar took the dogs back to finish off the rest.

"Did you notice the crosses just back in the bush there, Harry?" said Campbell.

"No."

· 135 ·

"Albert showed me. It's Frank and Willie McLeod and their partner, Weir."

"First name?"

"None. No one's ever been able to trace him, even though Charlie McLeod says he worked at the post in Fort Providence. Charlie also claims that Weir isn't actually buried there."

Faille laughed. "Charlie's some poet. Goes to seances, talks to the dead, works his Ouija board. A while back, he claimed to have tracked Weir to some Alberta homestead. Weir got the drop on him but wouldn't shoot, said he had enough regrets about killing Frank and Willie. He climbed on a haystack, lit it on fire and shot himself in the head."

"A damned ingenious way to end the story," said Vandaele. "Weir kills himself and gets rid of any evidence at the same time!"

"Like I said, Charlie can spin a yarn. His problem is that he wants to have it both ways. Not long ago he decided to resurrect poor old Weir. He got the Edmonton police to detain some guy who turned out to be a local farmer just trying to have a quiet beer in the Corona Hotel."

A couple of hours later, they left the Meilleur, crossed the Nahanni and pulled into shore just below the last gravel outwash of the Prairie Creek delta. Clark and Lomar stayed with the boats, and the rest ascended what Faille called Dry Canyon on a well-used sheep trail. The trail led to a ridge overlooking a gorge that was neatly divided by crumbling rock walls, so that it looked like the catacombs under a long-gone cathedral. At the end of the ridge they descended a narrow gully that ended abruptly at the edge of a cliff. They stood silently, looking down into First Canyon.

A thousand feet below was an island; the main part of the river flowed between it and the south wall. Blocks of ice and broken trees were piled at the island's upper end, but otherwise the canyon was clear.

"We have to avoid that far wall," said Faille, pointing. "There's a rock up against it, around the bend, and big waves go from the rock clear out to mid-river. Swing close around the far end of the island and go through tight against this side."

They managed First Canyon with no difficulty, and by dusk they were turning into the Liard River and pulling up to the Mulhollands' little dock at Nahanni Butte.

Daisy Mulholland gave them coffee, sandwiches and pie. In exchange, they handed over most of their moose. It would have been a happier time if Daisy and Jack hadn't looked worried, if Bill and Joe had been there.

"We saw signs of them," said Faille, "at the mouth of the Flat. I figure they could've rafted to the portage around First Canyon and they're still walking the trail. Or if they made it past the canyon and rafted into the splits, we could've passed them anywhere if they were in a different channel. We could go up and look, Jack. We could take my canoe and use your motor."

Mulholland agreed. "I appreciate that, Albert."

"The funny thing is, Dal dropped them at Glacier Lake instead of Rabbitkettle," said Clark. "Did you know that, Jack?"

"Dal never mentioned it when he came in to sell his pelts."

"Glacier Lake is just above Rabbitkettle Lake, to the

north," said Zenchuk. "It's fed by a big icefield. There's an old cabin there too, and the trapline's better marked. Dal might've flown them over for a look, and they decided to try it."

Faille sold his pelts, taking part of his payment in groceries and a new outboard, all of which he would pick up on his return in the summer. He wanted to go back in early, as soon as his old kicker was fixed in Fort Simpson and he'd stitched a new canvas skin onto his canoe. He was going prospecting, this time above the falls.

"I don't know what Dal will want to do with our pelts," said Zenchuk. "If he finds a load of freight or passengers in Fort Simpson, he'll trade them here or there. If not, he'll make more if he takes them straight to Edmonton."

"Fine, Nazar," said Mulholland. "That was a good load you brought in last month. With that and Chief Charlie's catch, and whatever Bill and Joe bring in, we're all right for another year. The Turner brothers are dealing their pelts here too. They're having a fight of some kind with Northern Traders."

"Didn't they just have a fight with the Hudson's Bay Company?" asked Zenchuk.

Mulholland smiled. "We're all they got left."

With the noise and dangers of the river behind them, they slept well at Jack and Daisy's, in the heated storeroom. The next morning, Faille and Jack Mulholland began loading the canoe for a search back up the South Nahanni.

Kraus, Lomar, Clark and Zenchuk steered the scow into the wide expanse of the Liard, heading downstream to Fort Simpson. Vandaele and Campbell, on their way down the

Liard to meet Fred Turner at his brothers' place across from the mouth of the Blackstone River, borrowed an old canoe and motor from Jack and Daisy, promising to send it back with the first group heading upstream.

"If Fred's not there," said Jack, "cross over to Dick and Vera's place. Stan had an accident, chopped his foot with an axe. He and Fred might be staying over with them."

42

SHORTLY AFTER THE Flat River trappers and prospectors left Nahanni Butte, Dalziel lifted off Landing Lake, his traps and outfit packed in the cache and his skis, pelts and dogs in the back of the Robin. He could see that there was no sign of life at Faille's cabin across from Irvine Creek, nor at Zenchuk's cabin at the Caribou River. They would be all the way out by now, digging into Whittington's sandwiches and pie, gulping his beer.

At the mouth of the Flat, Dalziel made a wide circle and headed north, aiming for the tower of mist that marked Virginia Falls on the Nahanni. Above the falls, he watched the riverbanks for smoke or any white canvas tarps or lean-tos in likely spots along the river.

At Rabbitkettle Lake he circled low over the remains of the Eppler-Mulholland cabin, looking for tracks, then landed and pulled into shore where the trapline trail started at the opposite end of the lake.

He tied the Robin to a bush and let his dogs out, ordering

them to scout. Then he took his rifle, called the dogs and started along the marshy shore. A half-hour later, he walked into the circle of charred trees and blackened logs. The place was exactly as he'd left it. His dogs circled around, following their noses into the bush in places, quiet.

Once again he stood on the cache ladder, looking through the burned trees at the lake, now sky blue in the sunshine with patches of sparkling white around the shore. He lifted Eppler's can of paint and roll of canvas out of the cache.

Inside the scattered logs of the cabin, small pieces of melted steel were piled together on the grey ground as if someone had picked them out of the rubble and placed them there. Those would be the remains of the fuel barrel. There were some indentations nearby, footprints possibly, but so erased by spring meltwater and rain that he couldn't be sure.

Dalziel threw the door and door frame onto the ashes of the cabin and burned them, then scattered the charred remains in the bush. He walked the north half of the line, collecting the traps in a bag. On his way back past the cabin, he picked up the paint, canvas and pieces of steel, carrying it all around to the Robin. Then he lifted the traps from the south part of the line. In the heavy spruce about a mile up the Rabbitkettle River from the lake, he found some half-eaten carcasses by the side of the trail, a couple of marten and a fox, it looked like. Someone had to have dumped them there. Maybe they were some of the catch that Eppler didn't get to fast enough, before they got chewed on.

As he lifted off the lake and swung in a big circle, east,

then north, then west, picking up altitude, he pushed the door open and dropped the can of paint, the canvas and the pieces of steel into the forest. Then he flew up the creek to Wade's cabin at Glacier Lake.

Again, he pulled in at some distance from the cabin and got his dogs out to scout. He examined the cabin, which had burned down to two rounds. He climbed to the cache and stared at the pelts. Joe's and Bill's, he had no doubt. He dumped their traps into the cache near the bags of his own traps that Wade had never used. Then he left the lake, headed for the South Nahanni and flew low over it, looking for signs of life.

At the Butte he discovered from Jack and Daisy that what he feared was true: no sign of Bill and Joe.

"I just went up to the lake to check on them. The cabin burned, probably in late winter when the snow was still high. The bottom two rounds of logs survived the fire. There's a good three months' worth of pelts in the cache, and they pulled their traps before they left."

Daisy put her arm around Jack.

"They must have survived the fire and made for the river."

"No canvas? Paint?"

"No."

"Did you go through the remains of the cabin?"

Dalziel shook his head. "If the boys don't turn up soon, the police are going to want to poke around in it themselves. I watched the river on the way here, but I didn't see anything."

"It sounds like they came down the Nahanni, probably on

the water. The ice was going out when Faille and the boys got to the mouth of the Flat, and they found a fresh fire ring and cuttings there. Albert and I checked as far back as First Canyon. We covered some of the portage, too. There's a fire spot there, at the end of the portage, and fresh cuttings in the bush, but no sign of them anywhere. Some Indians could've come through, but we never saw or heard of any. Can you fly me in to look, Dal? I got the money."

"It won't cost you, Jack."

43

THAT AFTERNOON, JACK Mulholland pawed through the remains of the Glacier Lake cabin, turning up Eppler's fire-eaten lighter, the side lying on the ground still exhibiting the Macdonald's Scotsman. Checking into the cache, he also recognized the rope that the hides were tied up in, and affirmed that the hides were cut and bundled in Eppler's distinctive way.

They flew the pelts and traps out and Dalziel stayed at the Butte that night, taking off for Fort Simpson the following morning. He tied his plane to Faille's dock and walked the trail to town. Newton was in his office and Truesdell, fortunately, at the hospital.

"I heard that Bill and Joe haven't made it out," said Newton, as soon as he saw Dalziel. "I talked to Kraus and Zenchuk at Whittington's."

"I went to check and found the cabin burned down to

two rounds. I told Jack and went in again because he wanted to look. I just got back from taking him up. No one's moving on the river, no smoke coming up. We think they left their camp and made for the river. There's no sign of any human remains in the cabin."

"You dug around in it?"

"I told Jack he should wait, but he had to look. Can't really blame him. He found Eppler's lighter—he said Eppler never took it with him on the line. The fire wouldn't have been hot enough to burn up any human bones. Jack took the pelts. They were Eppler's for sure, cut the way Eppler did it and tied up with some rope that Jack recognized. There were enough pelts to show that they put in a good three months' work before the fire happened and they left. Their traps were all bagged and in the cache. Jack took them too."

"Any rifles in the ashes?"

"Nope. No one keeps them inside anyway, and they weren't in the cache."

"Probably they tried to walk out, then."

"More likely they made their way down to the river and built a skinboat. The canvas and paint weren't in the cache, and the river was probably open when they got to it."

"Does Jack want a search?"

"Yes."

"Can you fly me up?"

"Plane's still warm. I'll just have to gas her up. We'll stop and talk to Jack?"

"Certainly."

Newton started to say something, stopped and pointed at a piece of foolscap on his desk.

"Clark was here last week, registering a complaint. He saw wolf pelts at your camp."

"They raided my line."

"Do you have them with you?"

"Hell, no. But you can look."

"Normally we'd overlook it, but Truesdell will ground you for sure—he's tired of the fines. Frankly, Dal, the wolves are only an excuse. He'll figure he's saving lives by keeping you grounded. Maybe you don't want to fly me in now."

"You could commandeer the plane and me. Any planes due in?"

"MAS is bringing some stuff for us."

"Soon?"

"Tomorrow, day after tomorrow."

"Good. When Truesdell takes the plane, I've got a ride out. Want me to bring a couple of dogs?"

"Good idea."

4 4

A DAY LATER, back in Fort Simpson and none the wiser, having confirmed Dalziel's and Jack Mulholland's conclusions about what had happened, Newton prepared to meet Faille, Zenchuk, Kraus and Clark for an interview. He'd already prepared Dalziel's statement while they were at the lake.

There, he'd filtered through the cabin remains as best he could, though he had only a couple of rough implements—a trowel and a magnetic metal detector—to help. Dalziel assisted, but as the spoons, knives, melted pots, tin cans, jars and other domestic items piled up alongside what Jack had found, Newton sensed that Dal was getting impatient.

"This is all stuff you kept here?"

"Most of it."

Yet he and Dal had camped there overnight, making a fire near the cabin, and they'd shared some Scotch and swapped stories. Truesdell's experience was that Dal was hostile, but Newton saw none of that. When they discussed the pending debate on airplane trapping, and the issues of banning trappers from using their own planes, Dal calmly outlined his objections.

"Usually this country is empty. One or two parties of Indians might come through, trapping as they go, but most years Nazar and I have been the only ones around. Faille prospects above the falls, but he keeps his traplines down on the Flat. Airplane trapping will allow trappers with planes to come in here when the south gets too crowded. And if you passed a law keeping all the whites out of here, there'd be poachers coming into the upper Flat and the Rabbitkettle from the Yukon. There'd be nothing you could do about it."

"Not until we get our own plane. But trappers will always be able to use commercial airlines to come into this country."

Dalziel shook his head. "No trapper could afford the prices. All the profit would be gone."

"I guess that's true. There's no money for us police to fly around, even. But there *will* be a ban on airplanes, Dal. That's for sure. Truesdell and his friends in the government are convinced that competition with whites is driving the Indians off their traplines."

"It's the handouts that are driving them off, Regis. Everyone knows that."

Newton shrugged. "What will you do when you can't fly to your lines anymore?"

"I'll keep the ones in the Yukon and BC, for a while anyway. But I like hunting and fishing. I'll go into guiding and outfitting, apply for a designated territory somewhere and set up a flying base in Fort Nelson or Watson Lake."

"You think enough people have the money for that?"

"There are always people with lots of money. Most of the outfitters in Alberta are doing better now than before the stock market crash."

Now, Newton rifled through his desk, located his notepad and placed it in front of him. It was time to sum up. Not a death certificate, but in this country what usually amounted to the same thing: a missing-persons report.

As Newton added to his notes, the men arrived, chatting with one another. Newton realized that they'd caucused at Whittington's and walked over together.

As they removed their coats and sat, Newton greeted them from behind his desk. "I have to submit a written report, including witness comments. Basically, my report has to deal directly with what probably happened to the boys. But feel free to elaborate on any of the questions

I ask, or add anything you want to say, even if it doesn't seem important."

The four men nodded.

"So Dal definitely informed you, back in April when you visited his trapline, that the boys might be coming down Irvine Creek to Albert's cabin?"

Clark and Kraus nodded.

"And he told you the same, Nazar, and you reported that to Albert?"

Faille and Zenchuk nodded.

"What surprised me, though," said Clark, "was that the boys went to Glacier Lake instead of Rabbitkettle. Jack told me they were heading for Rabbitkettle Lake. Nazar assumed they were there."

"There's no doubt they were at Glacier Lake," said Newton. "Evidently they changed their minds on the way in. When Dal flew Jack up on a search, Jack saw right away that the pelts in the cache were Bill's. He told me that they were cut the way Bill did it, and bundled with some rope that Jack recognized. And he found Bill's lighter in the remains of the cabin."

"He was sure?"

"Absolutely. He showed it to me when Dal and I dropped in on our way upriver. An Export A lighter. You could still see the markings. Nazar, what did Dal tell you about Bill's plans for a skinboat?"

"Just that Bill and Jack both talked to some of the Indians camped at the Butte, and the Indians gave them an idea of how to put a skinboat together. Dal tried to talk

Bill into using a raft instead, or walking to Albert's by way of Irvine Creek."

"And that was good advice," said Faille.

"There was no canvas or paint in the cache," said Newton. "It could've gone up in the cabin fire, I suppose."

All four men shook their heads. "Eppler would know better than to put something essential like that in the cabin," said Faille.

Newton was silent for a couple of minutes, writing. "So it's likely they went at least partway out in the skinboat. But why would Eppler want to come out in a skinboat? Everyone says it was a crazy idea."

Faille nodded. "Jack told me once that Bill often did get hold of ideas like that, and once he got them he had to try them out."

"Did he or Joe know how to swim?"

Faille laughed. "Wouldn't do any good if they did. You got to stick with your boat no matter what. If you're on a raft, you got to tie yourself and your rifle to it. If you lose all your equipment, it would just be a longer and more painful way to go than drowning."

Newton wrote. Then he asked about the fire ring at the Flat River.

"It had to be them," said Zenchuk. "That fire spot wasn't there when John and I went in last fall, and we were the last ones in."

"That's John Lomar."

Zenchuk nodded. "He qualified for his licence and went up to Fort Norman to find his own line."

"And you're sure, Albert, that that fire spot and the one below First Canyon were fresh?"

"Positive. Jack was sure of that too, when we were there."

"So he told me," said Newton.

"Any sign of what might've caused the cabin fire?" asked Clark.

"Possibly the stove that Eppler rigged out of old kerosene tins. In fact, he started a small fire with it, in one of the walls, while Dal was still there helping them set up."

"Wasn't there a proper stove in the cabin? Why didn't they take one in?"

Zenchuk laughed. "They wouldn't have gotten up there with all their stuff and their dogs in Dal's plane if they threw a stove on the pile," he said. "Too heavy. Anyway, Dal probably tried to talk them out of using the cabin. He never uses cabins himself. He sees them as fire traps."

"He did try to talk them into taking a tent," said Newton. He wrote, tossed his pen down and looked up at them. "That's it. The report'll say they left their camp after a cabin fire, maybe caused by a faulty stove. The fire probably took place late in the season, since there were two complete rounds of logs left, probably because of snow piled high against the walls. Also they'd collected two or three months' worth of hides. I'll conclude that they likely drowned in the river or were lost in a slide or an overflow or avalanche while making their way out."

"No more searches?" Clark asked.

"I couldn't justify another one," said Newton. "But we will advise people to keep their eyes open."

"Could you extend your September patrol up to my place near Irvine Creek?" Faille asked. "In August, I'm going up Irvine and across the Rabbitkettle River just above the hotsprings. Got to prospect on some creeks up there. I'll camp at Rabbitkettle Lake, then head up to Glacier. I'll check around, but I won't be back here for a year to report."

"When are you leaving Simpson?" Newton asked.

"Soon as my scow's wrapped in new canvas. Nazar and Gus are going in too, to do some work on their camps. We'll have two scows, and I'll be helping Gus get his stuff up to McMillan Lake and start on a cabin. We agreed that we'd go right up to the falls, too, and check things out along the portage. They had to come down that way if they didn't go by way of Irvine Creek."

"We do our September patrol up to Fort Liard," said Newton. "Going up the Nahanni would be a first—there's never been enough population there to justify it. I'll try to get permission to hire a guide and go as far as your place, and see if you found anything."

"That'll make Jack and Daisy a lot happier," said Faille. "If I leave my cabin around then, I'll remember to put a note on the table."

"Tell me this," said Clark suddenly. "When are they going to shut Dal down? I mean permanently. It seems that Dal's not at fault in connection with Joe and Bill, but it's still damned dangerous to be dropping men into that country so far away from anything."

"You get dropped in every year, Bill," said Zenchuk

impatiently. "And this year you floated out and damn near died. We're all lucky to be here."

Newton lifted his hands. "Frankly, boys, the way Truesdell tells it, you're all finished, except Bill and Gus, who are strictly prospecting. Dal's operation is just a small part of it, though he sure stirred things up with that plane of his. They're going to ban all white trapping in those mountains, just like they prohibit the beaver hunt to whites some years."

"Our days are numbered," said Faille, grinning at Zenchuk. "We'll just have to move into the Yukon or BC."

"Dammit," said Kraus. "I like this country, and I'm just coming up for my licence. There's some good trapping around our camp at McMillan Lake."

Clark stood up, took his coat off the back of his chair and started to leave. The others followed suit, nodding their goodbyes to Newton.

"Anybody for a drink?" asked Kraus, once they were outside.

"I'm off up the river to Providence, boys," said Clark. "Then to Edmonton. Got to raise more money."

"I'll see you in September as usual," said Kraus. "We'll have a comfortable cabin by then. Don't forget to bring some whisky when you fly in."

Faille and Zenchuk wished Clark well and then moved off, with Kraus, in the direction of Whittington's.

"You don't seem worried, Albert," said Kraus.

"I never ran into a game preserve I couldn't get around," said Faille. "And there'll always be plenty of other things to do here."

As they entered Whittington's, Zenchuk said to Kraus,

"Marry up with one of them Indian ladies, Gus. Then you can work her trapline even when the mountains are closed to whites."

"By golly," said Kraus, "that's a good idea. Why haven't you done it, Nazar?"

"Never thought of it before. You know, Mary Littlejohn might've been giving me the eye when me and Dal flew her to Edmonton. Mind you, she was drugged up pretty good."

"We'd be real citizens. Too bad *you're* married, Albert."

Faille laughed. "Last I heard, anyway."

"When was the last you heard?"

"About five years ago," said Faille, suddenly serious. "We met in Edmonton. She came all the way from Pennsylvania on the train. I told her about the life up here. She said she'd think about it. I guess she's still thinking."

4 5

"WHAT THE HELL happened up there?" asked Zenchuk. He and Dalziel were in their tent at Fort Simpson, the Robin tied up, government property now, at the dock in front of Faille's cabin.

Dalziel considered. He and Zenchuk were well into a bottle of Scotch, one they intended to finish before the night was done. Then Dalziel would head to Yellowknife, site of a new gold strike, rumoured to be a big one. He'd look for summer work, maybe as a pilot with one of the mining companies that were moving in. Zenchuk would fix up the scow, get his outfit together and go back in to the Caribou River camp with Faille and Kraus.

"I figure Wade killed them, burned the cabin with the aviation fuel and took the hides. Maybe he stuck the bodies in the cabin before he burned it."

"*Why?*"

"You were probably right all along. Crazy. I think he killed and burned Czybek too, just before he walked into our camp on the Coal River."

"And it was Bill's lighter up at Glacier Lake?"

"No question, but Jack said Bill never carried the lighter out on the line. Wade must've taken it out of the Rabbitkettle cabin."

They sipped their drinks, sitting back on their chairs, feet up on blocks of wood in front of the stove.

"Wade would've had their rifles," said Zenchuk.

Dalziel nodded. "Gives me the sweats every time I think of it. I slept at our old camp at the other end of the lake that night. I guess the rifles were stashed well away from the cabin, and he couldn't get to them in time to come after me."

"Maybe. Or he decided to avoid you, because of the dogs. You said the wind was in your favour. And they tore his leg, so he might not have been moving around too fast. By God, Dal, he could still be up there. There's a chance he's still alive. We should tell Newton."

"Then Truesdell would have everything he wants to put me out of business for good. I could even lose my pilot's licence."

Zenchuk was silent. Then he said, "Wade would've gone

for the rifles, wherever they were. He would've heard you leave. He didn't get his groceries so he must've been low on food. Probably he went back to the cabin, found it burned and nothing to eat in the cache. Then he would've tried to get out fast before he starved to death."

"I think so," said Dalziel. "And I don't think he would've made it."

Zenchuk thought for a moment. "But we don't know that for sure. I was talking to Harry Vandaele. He says you're considering hiring him to work the trapline at the hotsprings. Don't do it, Dal."

"I could train Harry for a month or so, earn some money and take that time to make sure the area's clear."

Zenchuk shook his head.

"Harry's hot for an adventure," said Dalziel. "He wants to be on the Nahanni River, above the falls."

"Not when there could be a crazy killer in the area. Put him at Landing Lake."

"You worry too much. Even if Wade's alive, he's got no supplies. He'd have to move on or starve. Landing Lake needs to sit a year. The line at the hotsprings is ripe."

46

THE TORTUROUS DESCENT of the small river took three days. From time to time, Eppler watched from the forest edge as the killer ascended one of the many bluffs that slowed their progress, and Kubla sniffed up to some scraps of meat that had been gnawed and spat out, though these ended on the second day.

Eppler still hoped to weaken his quarry enough so he'd be tempted to surrender. Maybe that would happen when they got to the Nahanni, when the killer was forced to stop and make a stand or put a raft together.

If I can just get him alive, I can find out what happened to Joe, he thought.

Now the snowshoe tracks ended at bare gravel, a sweeping beach where the river Eppler was on widened into many channels and poured into the South Nahanni. Ahead, he could see an endless row of glittering chunks of shore ice. There were gaps in that wall, which would allow access to the river.

Kubla was picking up a trail heading south. In that direction, about a mile away, a low rocky bench, populated by spruce, crowded the shore. Eppler summoned him back and removed his saddlebags. He checked his rifle and poured shells into his pocket. The pack, toboggan and showshoes would stay behind.

"All right," he said.

Kubla moved ahead, nose down. Crossing the open wash would be dangerous, but now there was no choice.

They made it off the wide outwash of the small river and onto the boulder-ridden, ice-strewn shore of the South Nahanni. Where the shore ice was split, and there was driftwood, that would be the spot where the killer would get onto the river. Or at the forested bench; there would be plenty of dry spruce lying on the ground.

As the beach started to narrow around the forest, Kubla

edged toward a break in the ice. Then Eppler saw scrape marks on the sand and gravel. He whistled softly, and Kubla stopped.

"He's dragged some logs through there. He won't hear us over the river, but we got to be careful."

He came up along the ice to the break, and peered into it. It opened to the river, but there was a large boulder close to the water, obstructing his view of the shore.

Kubla, suddenly agitated, sprang forward, but Eppler reached down to grab him. As he did, the killer appeared around the boulder and raised his rifle. Eppler dodged back, and the shot blasted some ice above his head.

As soon as he let go of Kubla to grip his rifle, the dog dashed into the opening.

"Damn!" Eppler immediately poked his head and rifle around the ice. No killer, and Kubla was running for the boulder. There was a loud splash. Kubla disappeared around the boulder and Eppler tore after him, his gun shouldered. Another splash.

The man he'd been chasing, stretched on a puny raft, was spinning into the current. Kubla, not 10 feet behind, was swimming after him. The killer tried to bring his rifle up but the raft tilted violently and the rifle went down. Then, as the raft turned a slow full circle, the rifle came up again, pointing at Kubla.

"Not my dog too, you son-of-a-bitch," Eppler muttered, firing two shots, one at the killer's head and one, as the raft rotated, at his hip.

The rifle slid into the water. The raft whirled into some waves and vanished.

47

DALZIEL'S FLIGHT TO Yellowknife cost $100. Stan McMillan, the pilot, was apologetic.

"Sorry, Dal. I'd ride you for nothing, since you could end up doing me a favour sometime, picking me off an ice floe or a lake somewhere. But when we dock at Yellowknife, and they see it's *you* getting off, I'd damn well better have your full fare in my pocket."

"I understand. How do you like the Norseman?"

"The Pratt and Whitney is a bit sluggish for the payload—it's half a ton—but you know how it goes. The next motor will be a lot bigger."

As the Norseman dropped down onto the bay, Dalziel examined the west shore. Buildings were going up everywhere, and a tent city clustered around the rock outcrop. The gold was here, not up the Nahanni. If the discoveries continued, Yellowknife could be as famous as Dawson. He grabbed his bag and jumped out as the plane bumped into the dock. He went straight into Pete Ranch's log hotel, sat near the cash box and ordered a coffee.

Pete came out from the kitchen. "You just come in with MAS?" he asked.

Dalziel nodded.

"That's a switch. You didn't lose another assistant, did you?"

"I blasted four thieving wolves."

"Shame on you."

"So I'm looking for a temporary job until Truesdell sees fit to give me my plane back."

"You came to the right place. Consolidated has hired a hundred men since Christmas. They're building camps everywhere, and staking claims all around the damn lake."

"I'm no miner."

"I'll tell you what," Pete said. "Jack McNeill was in earlier. He's just bought two old Fokkers off United Air and he's going to try flying meat in here. Miners are a hungry bunch, and the stuff coming up from Edmonton isn't making anybody happy. I've had sausages and eggs blow up in my face. McNeill has one pilot hired straight out of flying school, a kid named Bernie Richardson, but he's going to need at least two more."

Later that day, Dalziel found McNeill.

"You'll be chief pilot, Dal. I've got Bernie, and Archie Vanhee is coming up from Edmonton to be his mechanic. You can sit beside Bernie on his first flight to Fort St. John. Then I'll put you on the run to Fort Liard."

The Fokkers were old and cranky, and the meat stank. The business went well, though there were grumblings from MAS and Canadian Air about how the authorities should enforce some meat-inspection rules.

One day in June, McNeill brought an old *Edmonton Journal* back from a business trip, and passed it to Dalziel.

"A couple of guys from Fort Simpson," he said. "Turns out they didn't come out this spring."

It was front-page news:

MISSING MEN

Fort Simpson, N.W.T., May 1936. RCMP in Fort Simpson are inquiring as to the whereabouts of two trappers, Bill

Eppler and Joe Mulholland, who failed to return from their trapline as arranged. In January, the two were flown to Glacier Lake to trap marten, lynx, and beaver. They took with them the materials for the construction of a skinboat and planned to paddle out with their catch after breakup and before high water. Other trappers coming out from the Flat River this spring found signs of Mulholland and Eppler as far down as the First Canyon of the Nahanni, but the men never arrived at the post at Nahanni Butte.

The South Nahanni River is a treacherous piece of water and can prove disastrous to those attempting to navigate it without suitable equipment. Others believed drowned on the river are Frank and Willie McLeod, whose remains were found in 1906 in Deadmen Valley. Martin Jorgenson went up the Nahanni looking for gold in 1912. His remains were found in front of his burned cabin near the mouth of the Flat River. Still others, Yukon Fischer (1927), Mary Lafferty (1926), Phil Powers (1934), and Donald Gilbertson (1935) have disappeared under mysterious circumstances in the area.

Dal handed the paper back. "They were working one of my lines."

"Why didn't you pick them up?"

"Because they didn't want to be picked up."

On his next meat run to Fort Liard, Dalziel encountered Harry Vandaele and Milt Campbell. They were on the dock putting tools, bagged groceries and coils of canvas hose into their canoe. With Harry's brother Joe and Dick Turner's brother Fred, they'd barged their force pump down the Fort

Nelson River into the Liard and were working some likely areas along the right bank.

"Not much gold yet," said Vandaele. "You still have that trapline for me?"

Dalziel nodded. "When will you be back in Simpson?"

"September or earlier. Sooner rather than later, by the looks of it."

"Use my tent. Nazar won't be there. He's going back to the Caribou River to do some repairs and lay out a new stretch of trapline."

48

SHORTLY AFTER DALZIEL and Vandaele talked in Fort Liard, Faille, Zenchuk and Kraus finished refitting their scows in Fort Simpson and started up the Liard. Faille picked up his groceries and new motor at Nahanni Butte. Then they turned into the Nahanni, making record time up the river to Faille's old cabin at the mouth of the Flat.

As they settled into a feast of bacon, beans and bannock, Kraus said, "We could use some meat, and I hear the sheep hunting's good on the slopes above the river. I'd like a nice head to put up in our new cabin at McMillan Lake. What do you boys think?"

Faille, who'd been waiting for someone to propose a bit of fun, sucked on his pipe and nodded. "Why not? We promised Newton we'd check the portage."

Next morning, Faille produced his favourite breakfast, a porridge of rolled oats and whole wheat flakes, with salt, tinned butter and seedless raisins thrown in. He served it in large bowls, laying a thick slice of cheese on top. Then he produced brown sugar and canned milk to finish it off.

After coffee, they repaired the cache and loaded the building materials and most of their groceries into it. They dragged Zenchuk's scow onto high ground and loaded Faille's for the 10-mile trip to Virginia Falls.

Faille told Kraus and Zenchuk to keep their paddles close. "You'll see Circle Eight from a distance. The riverbed rises fast there, through two elbows of rock that divide the current. Half of it carries on downstream and the other half makes a circle upstream and then turns down again. Where it turns it collects driftwood. The Indians call it the Rapid that Runs Both Ways, and it's the worst spot on the river. The current will push us toward the first elbow. Get ready to stroke like hell, and don't stop till I tell you."

Kraus knelt in the prow. Zenchuk's dogs lay around his pack, behind Kraus. Zenchuk sat in the centre, Faille's dogs and pack behind him. Keeping the two sets of dogs apart was essential; the teams tore into one another at every opportunity, though being in a scow settled them considerably. The packs and rifles were lashed tightly down and covered.

An hour later, they approached a pile of logs that extended from the bank to their right almost clear across the river. Faille pointed the scow at the end of the log jam. "Get ready to paddle," he shouted. As they passed the logs, Zenchuk and

Kraus saw towering waves between them and a rock bluff that jutted like a ship's bow into the river.

"Holy God!" exclaimed Zenchuk.

They plowed through a six-foot crest and toward another, spray hitting them hard in the face, the outboard going full bore. Zenchuk and Kraus plied their paddles hard, not often finding solid water. Faille aimed left, through another wave, the scow coming to a near standstill, and then swung sharp right, along the edge of a whirlpool toward an elbow that would turn them upriver again. The river rose fast here, levelling off only after they were well around the elbow.

"You can rest now, boys," Faille shouted, throttling the outboard down.

"By God, Albert," said Kraus. "I'm glad you were with us on that one."

"Wouldn't have thought it was possible," said Zenchuk.

"You can thank that new kicker of mine."

A half-hour later, he pulled into a small eddy behind an old slide, a pile of rocks that had tumbled into the river after clearing a narrow swath through the forest. The sun beat straight onto the rockpile, drying their clothes and hair and making them sweat. They worked quickly to unload the dogs and empty the scow, then carried it and their stuff toward the trees at the bottom of the slide.

"Hot here," said Kraus.

"It'll stay that way until evening," said Faille. "But we won't be back until late or maybe even tomorrow if the rams outsmart us. Let's tie up the dogs and get our food hung."

Soon they were hoisting their packs, shouldering their

rifles and starting up the slide. There, it was even hotter than on the rockpile, and the path upward was steep. The ground was dented with sheep tracks and covered in droppings, and they also saw the fresh prints of a grizzly. Their feet slipped out from under them regularly, sending down noisy avalanches of loose stones.

Finally they made solid ground, a hillside covered with birch, jackpine, silver spruce and low-bush cranberry. The grade became easier. Higher still, the bush gave way to alpine meadows, fragrant with sage. They dropped their packs and stood staring back down at the river, now a placid-looking ribbon of blue far below.

"Not much of a breeze, but God, does it feel good," said Zenchuk.

"Look at that funny cloud over there," said Kraus, pointing north at an unmoving mountain of white mist.

"That's the falls, Gus," said Zenchuk. "I've seen 'em from the air."

"Can we go up for a look?"

"Patience," said Faille. "We'll pass right in front of 'em tomorrow or the day after. You'll get the best view from there."

They angled upward, the slope levelling out, in the general direction of the falls. Then Faille, in the lead, stopped, turned, put his fingers to his lips and pointed at the horizon. There, Kraus and Zenchuk could see some dead wood on the ground.

Except there were no trees around.

The wood moved.

It was, Kraus and Zenchuk realized, a noble set of Dall sheep horns.

Faille lowered his pack carefully, cocked his rifle slowly and crept forward like a cat, his moccasined feet making no sound. At about 30 yards, the sheep suddenly sprang up and faced him, white against the gravel slope.

Faille fired. The ram stood, staring at him. Faille fired again. The animal plunged sideways and down, disappearing over the hill. Faille ran. Kraus and Zenchuk dropped their packs and ran after him.

"Pray God the ram doesn't drop into some canyon," said Zenchuk.

They topped the hill and found Faille and the ram in a grassy hollow.

"Those horns are a good yard or more on the outside curl," said Faille, kneeling beside the ram's head.

"You got him right by the eye," said Zenchuk.

"That must've been my second shot. I aimed for the neck the first time, reckoning not to damage the head. Didn't know if I'd hit him or not, though. He just stood there looking at me."

"It's them red pants you got on. The ram never seen anything like that before."

"If that's it, I'll wear 'em whenever I hunt."

Faille began to bleed his animal.

"Rams hang around in bachelor clubs," said Kraus. "Let's have a look."

Kraus and Zenchuk walked quietly through the hollow and up to a rocky knoll. From there, they saw three magnificent rams standing like statues on the next knoll, all gazing into the blue mountains far away on the other side of the river.

"You take the one to the right," whispered Kraus. "I'll get the one on the left. Then we'll both go for the middle one. He'll probably jump."

Four shots rang out, and all three rams collapsed where they stood.

A couple of hours later, they had the meat and the biggest head—from one of the three rams shot by Kraus and Zenchuk—carried down to a patch of spruce and willow. They built a platform on the ground and stacked half the meat onto it, shading it with spruce boughs. After the rest of the meat was loaded into their packs, they started down, Kraus cursing his ram's head, which, tied to the outside of his pack, seemed determined to butt him to death.

"What do you expect?" said Zenchuk. "You just shot the poor bugger!"

By the time they got to the bottom they were hot, blood-covered and bug-bitten. Luckily, the shadow of the forest was now across the rockpile, and the evening chill was setting in.

"We'll cut up the meat and smoke it tomorrow," said Faille, "once we're settled on the other side. Up early when it's still cool and up the hill again for the rest of the meat, then across the river and out of this oven."

Faille fed the dogs almost half the meat they'd packed down the hill, and prepared a dinner of sheep's liver and bacon, with bannock and marmalade, while Zenchuk and Kraus built a little rock wall between two spruce. This would shade the meat the next morning. Kraus started to strip the ram's head. Zenchuk, noticing flies drifting toward the meat, lit smudge fires on either side, collecting piles of green willow to throw on them.

After dinner, Kraus prepared the head that he planned to mount in his new cabin. He took the skin cape he'd removed from the head and stretched it inside out on a paddle. He rubbed salt into it, then inserted a stick through the ears to spread the skin for drying. By the time he finished, hanging it and the skull between the smudges, Zenchuk and Faille were rolled into their lean-tos under their mosquito netting, sound asleep.

49

NEXT MORNING, FAILLE, Kraus and Zenchuk scrambled up the slide again, rifles slung over their shoulders and loaded in case the resident grizzly had got wind of their sheep. If he had and wouldn't budge, he would pay the price, though it would be no great advantage to their larder. Bears were good mostly for fat, and for fat they had to be shot in the fall.

No grizzly. They bagged the sheep meat and returned to camp, arriving just as the sun was beginning to heat things up.

"Blast it," said Zenchuk. "Let's get off this rock."

Once they were launched, Faille started laughing about their three inches of freeboard as they crept against the current. Soon they could hear a muffled roar, and the walls around them seemed to vibrate with it. Then they entered a cloud of fine mist. They moved slowly past a couple of sandstone cliffs and Faille announced, "We're here!" He kept as close to the shore as he could, crossed an eddy at the base of the last cliff and plowed straight into a riffle around the eddy's edge. Zenchuk and Kraus didn't have to be told to paddle. They broke through into the smooth water beyond the riffle, a small lake, at the side of which hung a high, surging white curtain. Gigantic fists of water pounded onto the rocks below and exploded upwards like geysers. Faille steered through the mist across the pool toward the other bank.

In a few minutes, they pulled into a small stone beach between house-sized boulders that had obviously, in some previous age, come off the falls. The beach was the terminus of the portage trail. Everything was covered in a fine slime, distilled out of the mist.

They released the dogs, unloaded the scow, dragged it up onto shore and grabbed the bags of sheep meat. Just off the river was a small campground with a few fire rings and some crosspoles for hanging food. Some of the poles were broken in the middle and hung down at crazy angles.

"Who made this place?" asked Kraus.

"The Klondikers. They went right up to Mount Wilson at the head of the Nahanni, then crossed over into the Pelly River or the Macmillan and on to the Ross and the Yukon. Don't know who gave them that fool idea, but you see signs of them all up the river. You'll notice corduroy on the climb around the falls. That was so they could skid their boats up."

They built a fire, set up some drying frames and smudges and started slicing the meat as thinly as possible, draping the strips over the frames. That done, they ate a heavy midday meal of sheep steaks. Then Zenchuk and Kraus, with Zenchuk's dogs, headed for the climb around the falls; Faille stayed back to keep the smudges going and turn the meat.

Within half an hour, they reached the top of the falls and stood on a slab of rock, watching the water go over the drop.

"Holy," shouted Kraus. "Imagine if you missed the portage and got caught in that."

Zenchuk made a slashing movement across his throat. They made their way along the shoreline to the top of the portage, about a half-mile above the falls. The river dropped dramatically in that distance, and the limestone channel was smooth and steep on both sides. Faille had referred to this stretch as "the chute." There would be no way out of it.

"Looks like Bill and Joe got off the river," said Zenchuk, pointing.

Kraus sifted through the unburned scraps of wood in the fire ring.

"Pretty fresh, all right."

50

IN MID-SEPTEMBER, HARRY and Joe Vandaele, Milt Campbell and Fred Turner gave up on the gold-washing experiment and took the barge back up to

Fort Nelson. Joe Vandaele went home from there, while the other three retraced their route down the Fort Nelson River to the Liard. Down the Liard, Campbell would check in at the Netla River and maybe begin his winter's work with an established trapper, Boo Judah. Fred Turner would join his brother Dick and sister-in-law Vera on their trapline just down the Liard from Boo's. Vandaele would continue to Fort Simpson to meet Dalziel, in the hope that he would have a trapline available.

The trip down the Fort Nelson and into the Liard revitalized all three men, lifting them out of their sour feelings about prospecting. One afternoon, still on the Fort Nelson, they shot a moose from the canoe. It was standing conveniently on a gravel bar, a good camp spot. They cleaned the moose, hung it, made camp and tucked into some steaks garnished with fresh potatoes and carrots, a donation from a proud gardener in Fort Nelson.

"Dammit!" said Vandaele, after they'd silently put back the first serving. "I've given up on gold, I swear. Never again will I be led by that false promise! But I'm still determined to stay in this country. I like this life better than anything I've done before."

"Which is, to be precise," said Campbell, "shovelling manure out of your dad's barn, and pumping gas and selling cars in Calgary. Hardly a wide sampling of human experience, Harry. How about getting more education? Maybe you could be a teacher, or a doctor. Or a lawyer. That's how I see you. A fancy suit. You looked good in a suit, back when you were selling cars. You'd have an office lined with books. You like books. You could go from law into politics. You give good speeches. You can talk people into any kind of foolishness. Me, for example."

"Don't make me depressed, Milt. You know I go funny when I'm depressed."

"I'd fancy a steady job, myself," said Campbell. "Around here, if possible."

"Not possible," said Turner. "If you're not an Indian, if you haven't worked your way up in the Hudson's Bay Company or joined the RCMP, you're on your own."

"What did you do before, Fred?" asked Vandaele.

"Shovel manure out of my father's barn. My brothers persuaded me to come up here. That was two years ago."

"And?"

"I want to go back to farming, when things start to look up. I'm already dreaming of my cozy bedroom, Mum's cooking and our Marconi radio."

"With a choice of Cajun, Nashville or Carnegie Hall, depending on reception," said Vandaele. "I dream about that too, but farming's not for me."

"We might as well have some fun," said Campbell. "There are no jobs anywhere, and the farms are all dried up. We're on an extended vacation. We're exiled, stranded. And most of the talk back in civilization is about a war. If that happens, this place could look like paradise."

"I admire Dalziel," said Vandaele. "Look what he's done in only a couple of years."

"You're not like Dalziel," said Campbell. "You're a dreamer. That's one of the things I like about you."

"Never met him," said Turner, "but he's a hero to Dick and Stan. Dick even talks about getting a plane someday."

The next evening they pulled into the mouth of the Netla and camped by Boo Judah's cabin. Learning that Vandaele and Campbell had their own scow, Judah gave Campbell a list of supplies and groceries to pick up at Fort Simpson and bring back to the cabin.

They carried on the next morning, dropping Fred off at Dick Turner's place on the Blackstone River. Stan Turner, they learned, was down at Fort Simpson getting some treatment for his foot, which was not healing properly. Dick and Vera were building a root cellar to hold the bounty of a thriving garden.

Farther down the Liard, at the Beaver Dam Rapids, they helped pull a scow and launch, the *Muriel*, up the side of the river, earning a good meal with coffee and two dollars each. They camped just at the top of the rapids.

"So you're hoping Dal will put you somewhere on the Nahanni?" Campbell asked as they lit their last cigarettes before climbing into their bags.

"It's that river, Milt. I have this feeling that there's something waiting for me up there. But I could as easily get stuck on a trapline somewhere else. You got some concerns?"

"Wherever Dal puts you, his lines are a long way from anybody, and I've noticed your back's been bothering you."

"If it hits me bad I'll stay in camp and keep a hot fire going."

"I should live to see that! You work until a job's done, no matter what, just like your mum and dad. And what if Dal can't come in to get you?"

"Go easy on me, Milt. I've got to do something. My only option now is going back to Spruce View and holing up on the farm with my tail whipped."

"Not your only option. What about that girl you met in Yellowknife, Snyder's daughter? I hope you've noticed that I've been discreet about her. No jokes, not even a mention to Fred or Joe."

"You've been admirable, and I'm especially glad you kept her from Joe. He's near her now, and he has a grudge against me. I know him. The little bugger is capable of anything."

"She wouldn't go for Joe. He's a farmer. You did write her, didn't you? After all those letters waiting for you at Fort Nelson?"

"Twice."

"You committed some of those nocturnal ravings to paper, I hope. They'd be just the thing to convince a young lady."

"I don't rave at night, Milt. What do I say?"

"It often ends in something like, 'don't shoot,' I think. Not that I deliberately listen, you understand. I assume that 'don't shoot' is a reference to her filmmaking activities, rather than her father."

"McMeekan made it pretty clear that Snyder would likely kill me and mount my head if I ever tried to carry her off. But I like a challenge."

"That's my friend talking, the Harry I know and love. If you need help courting her, count me in. Dorothy Snyder could be the gold mine we've been looking for."

"I'm gonna miss you this winter, Milt."

51

D A L Z I E L   Q U I T   H I S job at the end of September and rode out with Bernie and Archie to Fort Simpson. The Robin was still tied at Faille's dock, and there was no sign that Harry had been living in the tent.

Dalziel dumped his pack and walked over to Whittington's.

"Come for your plane?"

"Sort of. What do you think my chances are?"

"Maybe it don't matter anyway. Look what just came in."

Andy handed him an *Edmonton Journal*, folded open to a headline on page 3:

TRAPPING BY AIRPLANE FORBIDDEN BY OTTAWA

Inroads of White Men Into Fur Trade of North Inflicts Hardship on Indians, Commons Is Told.

Ottawa, September 21, 1936. Airplane trapping in northern Canada has been forbidden, Hon. T. A. Crerar, Minister of Mines and Resources, told the House of Commons as he gave an outline of plans his department has for betterment of conditions among Canada's 112,000 Indian population.

Relief costs among the Indians in the last fiscal year were $1,000,000 and this is due in a measure to their abandonment of their old vocations for fur trapping. And the inroads of the white man are accountable to some extent for this.

One white trapper obtained a pilot's licence and bought an airplane with which he was able to cover traps over an area of 125 miles. Discouraged Indians in that district have given up trying to compete with him but this form of trapping is now forbidden.

It is hoped areas can be set aside exclusively for the exploitation of Indian trappers, adjacent to the Indian reserves, that Indian tanning and leather working, basketry and wood carving can be marketed more advantageously for them and the Indian population can be placed on a more independent basis.

Canada's one "flying trapper," George Dalziel, who spent the previous trapping season up the headwaters of the Nahanni River, in a country little frequented even by Indians, may find his present enterprise ended by the government's new ruling.

Use of the plane in trapping is less for the purpose of covering a trapline than of scouting out new trapping territory. It was Dalziel's practice to seek out virgin areas, from which furs were not being drawn by other trappers, white or native, friends state.

Dalziel makes his headquarters in Edmonton. He learned to fly two years ago at the Edmonton Aero club and bought a Curtiss-Robin plane which he uses to fly to his trapping grounds and carry out his furs.

—Frank Peebles

Dalziel brooded over the article, pondering the meanings behind the words. He noted that Peebles was loyal, fudging the truth considerably in saying that the plane was used more for scouting than trapping.

One thing was clear: the ban on airplane trapping was just

a start. "Areas adjacent to reserves" probably meant most of the Northwest Territories.

"Basketry," Dalziel muttered under his breath. "Wood carving."

Andy was still watching him when Dalziel looked up from his paper.

"What else is new, Andy?"

"I was in Vancouver a few weeks ago, visiting my sister. I saw Eppler downtown, going by in a taxi. I swear to God, Dal. With that pug nose and those funny sunglasses of his, I'd know him anywhere. He looked straight at me."

"Did you tell Regis?"

"He's out on patrol, but I told the doctor. You know what Dick figures? The boys found gold up there at your lake. They fought over it and Bill killed Joe and lit out. Remember how he was always talking about pulling up stakes here and finding gold in Australia? Having a good suntan all year 'round? I'll bet that's where he was going when I saw him in Vancouver."

"I know two sure things, Andy. Dick doesn't like Bill, and Bill wouldn't kill Joe."

"But it could've been an accident. You know how hot-headed Bill can be."

"I guess if you saw him, then something funny must have happened up there."

"I saw him. Where you going?"

"To the wireless."

"About your plane?"

"How'd you guess?"

52

VANDAELE TURNED UP the next day. Dalziel encountered him at the dock, seeing Campbell off with the load of supplies for Boo Judah's.

"Hope you have a line for me, Dal," said Vandaele. "I'm flat broke and none too popular with my friends and family. Our little pile of flour gold didn't even pay for use of the pump."

"Let's go up to the tent."

Vandaele settled his pack on a bed while Dalziel poured coffee.

"I've got the line, Harry. But there's a problem. My plane's still in the hands of the police. Also, it looks like I can't use it anymore to run my own traplines."

Dalziel showed Vandaele the newspaper.

After reading the article, Vandaele said, "We could still get up there in a scow."

"That would take two or three weeks, and I'd have to come back out. It would be worth it if I were thinking of trapping somewhere up there, but I've got other plans. I've figured out another way, though, if you're willing to play along with me."

"You bet I am. Is what you have in mind legal?"

"I'm not sure."

"That makes it even more interesting. What are we going to do?"

"Here it is. Andy's just back from visiting his sister in Vancouver. He swears he saw Bill there, in a taxi. Says he couldn't have been mistaken. Bill looked right at him."

"Andy's a nice guy, but one hell of a bullshitter."

"I'll say, but he told Truesdell, and he's collected a lot of believers, like Dick and Stan Turner. Dick figures that Bill and Joe found gold up there. They fought over it and Bill killed Joe."

Vandaele laughed. "And I thought I had an imagination. But everyone knows that Dick doesn't like Bill. I've never heard what's behind it."

"They had an argument, that summer that Kraus was talking about when Eppler returned the bucket of lard. Dick and Bill had gone in together to check their claims on McLeod Creek. As soon as they got there Bill wanted out, claiming he'd run out of tobacco. Dick raised a fuss, but Eppler insisted. So out they went, missing the chance to spend a month prospecting. Dick never forgot."

"That would make me mad too."

"But it goes back farther. When Dick and Stan first came to this country, they didn't know anything. They dropped in at the Butte to ask around, and met Bill. He sent them to Boo Judah. They worked all winter and came out owing Boo money for what they'd eaten. Lack of experience, and totally Boo's fault because he's well known for not teaching his assistants enough. But the Turners blamed Eppler. It could be that Dick, once they got to McLeod Creek, started nagging Bill, and Bill got fed up and wanted away from him."

"So Dick's still getting his digs in."

"Yes. But it's good for us. Here's what we do."

53

VANDAELE AND DALZIEL left the tent together, Vandaele for Whittington's and Dalziel for the wireless office, where the day before he'd left a message for his lawyer. He didn't like dealing through Isbister, the army captain who ran the office: Isbister and his wife were friends of the Truesdells. All four associated regularly with the Cooks, the Anglican pastor and his wife, and the Crees, who ran Northern Traders. They entertained one another through the long winters, mainly with dinners. Also they had a book club and a debate club of which they made up full membership, although Andy Whittington regularly succeeded in crashing the meetings.

But there was a message waiting. "FIRE LIT UNDER JUDGE STOP FRIEND TERRITORIAL COMMISSION APPLYING OXYGEN STOP"

Vandaele was established at a table at Whittington's with Stan Turner and Tiny Gifford, the local teamster.

"It's the mystery man," Turner said when Dalziel sat.

Dalziel arched his eyebrows questioningly.

Turner leaned toward Dalziel. "We just heard from Andy that getting information from you is like plucking a cold chicken."

"And that there's as much promise in asking you questions as there is in a bull humping a haystack," added Gifford.

"All this being in reference to?"

"Your plane."

"That's no mystery. They've got it, I don't. How's your foot, Stan?"

"I can walk from here to the door without crutches, and Doc says I'll be able to burn the damn things in a month. But Lord, does it ache at night."

"Good thing Dick was around when you did it."

"Yeah. And Vera. Truesdell said she treated it better than he could've. If I'd been trapping where you trap, Dal, I'd be long dead by now."

"A victim of the Nahanni."

Whittington came out of his kitchen with a plate of sandwiches. "Howdy, Dal," he said. "Getting your plane back?"

"No."

"Too bad. The boys and me were thinking. Something happened to Joe and Bill that needs investigating. Regis ain't gonna do it, because Truesdell won't give him the go-ahead. And this morning I learned something else. Remember Ernie Wainman?"

"Had a good trapline up the Mackenzie a bit. Got gold fever and headed down to Dease Lake."

Whittington nodded. "He stayed over last night on his way back upriver. Guess what he saw when he was saying his farewells at Telegraph Creek?"

"What?"

"Eppler's dog. One of those big Newfies Bill likes because he says huskies scrap too much and it gets on his nerves. You can talk to a Newfie, he always said. The dog turned up in June. The teacher found it tied up in front of her house with a note on its collar saying that the undersigned, except the note wasn't signed, had to go out, and the dog needed a new home. The teacher took it in, too. Know why?"

"Never met the woman, Andy. A dog lover, I suppose."

"There were a couple of nuggets rolled up in the note. Word is they were big ones, too. We figure Bill and Joe hit pay dirt."

"Most prospectors carry a couple of nuggets for luck. Or he could've panned them anywhere on his way out."

Turner leaned forward. "Maybe. And maybe he found them up the Nahanni. We figure to petition Truesdell to release your plane for the purpose of a proper search. It has to be done now, before winter."

"That's right," said Whittington. "You fly in with Harry here and check that whole area around Glacier Lake, down to the Nahanni. Check Rabbitkettle Lake too. Maybe they headed there after their cabin burned. Maybe that's where they found the gold. Albert's been going there regularly in summer, and he says he's found some promising creeks."

"Fly in with Harry?"

"Everyone else is busy," said Whittington. "Stan here can't walk, and Harry says he'd be happy to do it. We already wrote it up."

Vandaele patted his shirt pocket. "Got it right here."

"I'll sign it now," said Dalziel.

"We thought about that, Dal," said Whittington. "Harry figures you're the one person whose signature shouldn't be on it, and we agree. It's a conflict of interest. Also, Truesdell has a hernia whenever he hears your name."

So Dalziel stayed in his tent while Vandaele and Turner

spent the day acquiring signatures, going door to door, Stan, still on crutches, stumping along gamely. Everyone signed— the two Catholic priests, all 10 of the Gray Nuns, the Cooks, Crees and Isbisters, the two soldiers who helped Isbister in the radio office, Whittington, Gifford and a number of Indians who made their marks, Vandaele and Turner writing the names alongside the marks.

The petition read:

"We the undersigned request that George Dalziel's plane be released for the time it takes to search for Bill Eppler and Joe Mulholland up the Nahanni River. We will take all responsibility if there is a question of the legality of Dalziel breaking the seizure of his aircraft for the purpose of the search."

The next day, the petition was delivered to Truesdell, who shrugged and gave permission for Dalziel to fly in on another search.

Dalziel checked the plane over and started it while Vandaele and Gifford went to Northern Traders and picked up enough supplies, on Dalziel's account, for two or three weeks, the time that had been suggested by Vandaele as necessary for a thorough search that would include both lakes and the area between. Vandaele and Dalziel had decided to pick up more supplies at Nahanni Butte, in order to avoid suspicion. It was a good decision: even Truesdell joined the crowd that gathered to watch them load and wish them luck.

Dalziel allowed the plane to drift out into the current, then took off upstream, the people on shore waving.

Vandaele started to laugh. "You're good, Dal. As Andy might put it, the plan went down easier than a rum toddy on a cold day."

54

AT MULHOLLANDS' POST, Dalziel purchased, again on his account, bags of flour, sugar, rice and coffee, a coil of rope, rolls of canvas and wire, stovepipes, two five-gallon tins of kerosene, a half-dozen snares, a toboggan and some dog packs. He sent Vandaele over to the Indian campground to pick up a couple of dogs; he came back with two middle-aged huskies, Lisa and Maverick.

"The lady told me they were pretty docile," Vandaele reported. "That's the kind I like."

"As long as they can drag a toboggan and carry their 20 pounds."

Mulholland produced some food for the dogs, an aging haunch of moose from his cache, enough to last a couple of weeks. No charge.

"You staying in a long time?" he asked.

"Just between us, after we do the search Harry's going to trap my line below the hotsprings. Mum's the word, Jack. The good doctor wouldn't approve. Nor would the RCMP."

"I heard that Truesdell got his damned law."

"If I come out in a couple of months with our first load of pelts, will you take them?"

"Darned right I will. Daisy and I have been talking about shutting the place down anyway. With Bill gone and all the talk of a game preserve, we figure we should get out while we're ahead."

"Speaking of Bill," said Vandaele, "have you heard Andy's news, Jack?"

"Everybody coming up the river is talking about it. Maybe Andy saw Bill or maybe he didn't. But Dick's got no business spinning a murder out of it. Bill's a friend of mine, a good friend, and I'd trust him with my wife, never mind my kid brother. I'm gonna tell Dick he'd better stop that kind of talk or take his business somewhere else."

Next they flew up the river, close to the ground, down in the canyons even, to the falls, Dalziel spotting for camps on his side and Vandaele on the other.

Above the falls, Dalziel pointed out two hairpin curves on the river. "That's where you go over to the headwaters of Irvine Creek. Aim for that mountain and keep to your right around it. You'll come to a string of small lakes that feed into Irvine. That's your escape hatch if something happens, your way down to Albert's."

"What about the pelts?"

"It's *your* pelt I'm worried about. Just leave everything in the cache and cover it. I'll figure out how to get the pelts."

"Like how?"

"I don't know. Fly them out to Nazar, maybe, and let him bring them out on our scow."

"What's that?" said Vandaele a short while later, pointing ahead.

"Steam from the Rabbitkettle hotsprings. This is where we land."

They came down on the South Nahanni facing upstream, turned and drifted back, pulling into a small beach just upstream from a little bluff. Vandaele jumped ashore with a rope and tied up to a tree.

"Let's make camp and light the fire for tea," said Dalziel. "It's going to be pitch-dark soon."

Vandaele shovelled dead leaves out of the tent foundation while Dalziel uncovered the cache, extracted the tent and stored the rifles. They assembled a frame for the tent, building in an especially sturdy crosspole.

"You hang your frozen carcasses from that," Dalziel explained. "It's got to be strong."

From the cache they retrieved the stove, a lightweight affair made of two kerosene tins wired tightly together and floored on the inside with a couple of layers of flattened stovepipe tin. A hole had been cut at one end, and the piece cut out had been wired back on to function as a door. Another hole had been cut for the stovepipe, the pieces of tin folded up to fit inside the pipe and hold it in position. They placed the stove on four flat stones at the end of the tent opposite the door, and then installed a new chimney through the metal ring in the roof of the tent.

"Don't leave this thing alone unless it's burned down to embers," said Dalziel as he stuffed the stove with dry spruce branches and lit it. They made tea and cooked a great pile of rice and bacon.

After they ate, Dalziel said, "Here's the plan. Tomorrow

we winch the plane up onto the beach, drain the oil and put on the skis."

"You'll be here that long?"

"I intend to make maximum use of this hard-won opportunity, Harry. This line's been sitting for a couple of years, so it'll produce a good haul of pelts. We'll be at least two weeks setting it up properly just on this side of the river. We'll fix the camps and cut some dead wood for each one. Then we'll build a raft, float over to the other side and set up there. While we're setting up the line, we can check the gravel bars on both sides for any signs of the boys. On that side, the line goes right up to a bar across from the mouth of the creek that comes down from Glacier Lake. If Joe and Bill built a skinboat, that's where they would've done it.

"After we've got the line set up, we can put out a few traps. I'll show you how to take the scent off them, and we'll bring in some catch. Then I'll show you how to clean and stretch the hides. While we're doing all that, we have to keep an eye out for moose and caribou. You'll need a good stash for the dogs, and some jerky for yourself."

"There's more to it than I thought. I really appreciate you taking all this trouble, Dal."

"Ultimately, it benefits me. I'll make some money over the next while. The shipment that Jack's agreed to take will net us each about $100 after expenses. If you have a good winter, we could each take away over $1,000 on top of that. You could come in on your own for another year if it's still allowed, maybe even two more, before we have to let the line sit. Did you bring something to read?"

"No. I thought about asking Andy for some books, but I figured he'd get suspicious."

"He certainly would have. I'll leave you mine when I go."

Dalziel hauled a small, thick book out of his pack and showed it to Vandaele. It was entitled *A Treasury of English Verse.*

"Poetry?"

"I liked poetry in school, and I've taken to it even more over the years. It's more concentrated. It gives me something to memorize and mull over when I'm on the line. My wife gave it to me, so take good care of it."

They turned in for the night, Dalziel reading his book. An hour later, he blew out the lantern.

55

O N T H E W A Y back from patrolling up the Liard, checking to see who was settling in for a winter's trapping, Regis Newton and Diamond'C swung into Nahanni Butte and spent the evening with Jack and Daisy Mulholland. Then, fortified with one of Daisy's pancake breakfasts and a river of strong coffee, they started up the Nahanni to meet Faille and find out if he'd learned anything at Glacier Lake.

Diamond'C was a soft-spoken but witty man who entertained Newton with stories about the people and places they saw along the way. When they were at an old campsite near the mouth of Mary's River, above Third Canyon, sipping tea around their evening fire, Diamond said, "You been quiet today, Regis."

"It's this river, Diamond. People described it to me, but it's nothing I could've imagined."

"Whites call these the Funeral Mountains. My people are scared in here too, do lots of mumbo-jumbo when they go through. Ghosts in here."

"I've read the case files about the McLeods and Weir. And Jorgenson and a teenaged girl named May. You were in on the search for her."

"That was 20 years ago. She was the cousin of Mary Field, who was married to Poole Field who had the post at Nahanni Butte then. This river here is named for Mary, and a creek farther on up it is known as May Creek. Me, Boston Jack, Chief Tetso, Big Charlie and our families were camped here. We lived in the bush all the time then, trapping along the rivers, and we only went to the trading post when we ran out of shells and flour. We woke up one morning and May was gone, so we started tracking her. She didn't take anything with her but her clothes, and we started to find those about two days from camp. That was July, and the mosquitoes were bad, so we worried. She walked in a straight line, that way, up Mary River. When she got up into the mountains she started going up and over any cliffs that were in her way. Some of them we were afraid to climb. We circled around and always found her prints on top. We kept going, shooting food as we went, until on the ninth day we were down to six shells between us. The tracks went on, but we had to turn around. That was close to the canyons around Deadmen Valley, and by then she couldn't have had anything on but moccasins. She used to stay a lot with Mary, and we figured she was heading back to the post to be with her. But she never turned up."

Later, Diamond said, "You haven't asked me about my name yet. Everybody asks about my name."

"Diamond?"

"Diamond 'C, as in the third letter of the alphabet."

"I just assumed your parents named you Diamond and the C is your middle initial and stands for Charlie, maybe."

"Nope. My parents named me Adam, and figured with that name you don't get no middle name."

"So you go by a nickname."

"Sort of. But I've registered it as my family name. The C is really see, as in 'I can't see.' But when I was young I didn't write much, so it was easier to use the letter."

"And the Diamond part?"

"When I was a boy in Telegraph Creek, there was a diamond rush. I don't remember how it got started, but all you had to do was whisper 'silver' or 'gold' or 'tin' and there was a rush."

"Just like now."

"You're smart, Regis. Anyway, this white prospector gets me aside one day and asks me if I ever seen any diamonds and I said, 'What's a diamond?' and he showed me his ring. 'Diamond, see,' he said. Whenever he saw me after that he'd hold out his pinkie with the ring on it and point at the ring and say, 'Diamond, see?' It got to be a joke with folks, and after a while a lot of people thought that Diamond See was my name."

"You were lucky. It's an interesting name."

"Then I called my son Diamond too."

"As in the number two?"

"Maybe you're *too* smart, Regis. When I decided Diamond'C would be our *last* name, like it's one word, I gave him a first name because white folks like that. So I'm Adam and he's Dudley Diamond'C. Sometimes we call him Deedeecee. He sure hates that."

Up the Flat at the mouth of the Caribou River they talked to Zenchuk, who had finished setting up five miles of new trapline and was now replacing his chimney and banging some rolled tin onto his gables. Making the place wolverine-proof, he explained.

"Last winter, they just about got in on John, by widening the hole around the chimney insert. He swears they must've worked on it in shifts over a few weeks, and only when he was away on the line. So I fixed all that. Albert almost died a couple of winters ago when a wolverine wrecked his cabin and got the last of his food."

Zenchuk told them that he and Kraus had found signs of a fresh camp at the falls.

"That fits with what we know so far," said Newton. "How long since Albert and Gus left you here and went up the river?"

"I've been here about three months," said Zenchuk. "They took the scow and a canoe Albert had stashed here. They planned to go straight up to the mouth of McLeod Creek and then pack Gus's building supplies into McMillan Lake. Albert was going to help Gus with the logs for the cabin, and then head up Irvine Creek to Rabbitkettle and Glacier to have a look around the lakes. He should be back by now."

At Faille's they found a note: "Up Irvine Creek fishing." It was dated the previous day.

Diamond'C said, "He's at the pond."

They crossed the river and drifted downstream to the Irvine Creek outflow, finding Faille's scow pulled up into thick bush at the start of a well-worn trail. They dragged their scow up beside Faille's.

Faille was at the low end of the pond. Already it was starting to ice over, though the centre was still open. Faille had a five-pound Dolly Varden cut up for the pan.

"Get one more, boys," Faille said, nodding toward an axe sitting on the ice just offshore. "My line's on the axe. Don't worry about bait. They're starving in there and they'll go for the hook. Really, we're doing them a favour by eating them. I'll stir up the fire."

After dinner, Newton mentioned the fresh camp at the portage. "Nobody else came down the river in the spring," he said, "so whatever happened to the boys must've happened below First Canyon, in the Splits. We'll have to give that whole area a closer look."

"Amos Singletree came down," said Diamond. "From the Pelly, I think, and down the Nahanni."

"Amos came through? I asked all over Simpson and as far as the Butte, and even posted a notice. No one said anything!"

"With his brother and their wives and kids. And Old Amos too."

"Why didn't anybody say anything?"

"Amos scares easy. He might've thought he could get in trouble."

"How, for God's sake?"

"Maybe he wasn't supposed to be on the river. You never know about the law. Or maybe he ate Eppler. His grandmother claimed to be Naha."

"What?"

"That's Slavey for 'Nahanni,' Regis," said Faille, smiling. "The Slavey thought the Nahanni Indians were headhunters and cannibals."

"Every tribe thinks that about every other tribe," said Diamond'C. "But if Amos ate any white guys, he would've told me."

"Damn it to hell, you guys. This is serious. That means those fire rings and cuttings you found along the river last spring were made by Amos and his family. But wouldn't you guys have seen them, Albert?"

"Not likely. You got your eyes on the river when you're coming out, and not much time for looking at scenery. And they'd be camping and hunting as they went, or on the big portage around First Canyon."

"Damn!"

"It gets even more confusing, Regis," said Faille. "When I went to Rabbitkettle and Glacier this summer, I found the cabin on Rabbitkettle Lake was burned too. Blown up, maybe, judging by how some of the logs were scattered and the trees burned all around."

"How would someone blow up a cabin?" Newton asked.

"A prospector could have dynamite."

"I don't think Amos would blow up any cabin," said Diamond. "I think maybe Old Amos built that one, in fact."

Newton shook his head. "There's no way of putting this together now. I'll have to stick with my original report."

"Too bad," said Faille. "Just between us, I think Dal knows something about Mulholland and Eppler that he isn't saying."

"Mystery man," said Diamond.

"Why do you think that?" asked Newton.

"Just a feeling," said Faille.

56

WHEN VANDAELE WOKE up, Dalziel was making coffee and mixing hotcakes.

"I gather from what Kraus said at Landing Lake that you know how to snare rabbits," said Dalziel.

"I was the family expert."

"Get a half-dozen snares out of the cache and put them around camp while I'm making breakfast. Just in case moose are hard to come by."

"Good idea. There's plenty of rabbits around this year. We've been tripping over them."

After breakfast they used a hand winch that Dalziel carried in the plane to crank the Robin up onto the beach, and Dalziel drained the oil. There was already a fringe of shore ice along the river.

"It could freeze hard along the shore at any time now," said Dalziel.

They cut some sturdy poles, pried the Robin up, removed

the pontoons and attached skis. "Now we'll rope the pontoons into those trees and tie them up. When breakup comes, in early June, this river can do anything. You'd best move camp before then."

"Where to?"

"That bench on the other shore."

"That high?"

"I'll show you."

As they secured the pontoons to a big poplar, Dalziel pointed up. "There's the reason we're doing this, Harry. See that dirt ring? Now look at the rings on the rest of the trees. Notice the clumps of leaves and tufts of grass and small twigs caught in the branches at that level?"

"Good God."

"Last spring's flood. Usually there's a five- or six-foot rise at the flood, nothing to worry about. But once in a while the ice will jam just downstream and the water will back up. I figure it came up 20 feet last year."

Back at camp, they shouldered their packs and picked up their rifles.

"You know not to put your rifle inside?" asked Dalziel.

Vandaele grinned. "I didn't tell you about that, did I?"

Downriver, the line ran for about 12 miles through fairly level country, the mountain ridges on that side being about a mile away. The last half was mainly muskeg, frozen solid already. They crossed three creeks, choked with ice but still rowdy. They cleared deadfall from the trail and around the sites used for the traps, and replaced any tomato labels that had been blown away by wind or stripped off by porcupines.

The dogs followed, carrying the axe, hatchet, swede saw, short-handled shovel and food.

Dalziel identified a campsite about seven miles from the main camp, on an elbow of the river. The frame for the tarp needed replacing. As they worked on this, Dalziel pointed out that camps on the line were always built close to stands of dead spruce; they felled a couple of these, sawed them to six-foot lengths and dragged them into the camp, where they propped them against some nearby spruce for future use as firewood. Then they moved on. At the end of the line they fixed up another camp, Dalziel indicating that there was also a good spot on the other side of the river with plenty of dry wood.

"These camps at the extreme end of the line don't get used too much," Dalziel explained. "But you need them in case of emergency, like a blizzard."

They made tea, cooked up rice that was seasoned only by salt and some crumbled cheese, and slept.

Back at the main camp by noon the next day, they found that Vandaele's snares had produced a couple of rabbits. While Dalziel lit a fire, Vandaele cleaned them, tossing the skins, entrails, heads and feet to Maverick and Lisa.

Dalziel took a bucket from the cache, went for water and began boiling it over a fire that he built between the tent and the river. He went into the spruce with an axe and came back with fragments of bark, which he threw into the bucket, followed by a few dozen traps.

"The tannin in the bark takes the human scent away," he explained.

Then he and Vandaele made tea and turned their rabbits on a spit until they were done. They ate the rabbits with rice.

"Let's hope we get a moose soon," said Dalziel, tossing a rabbit bone to the dogs and frowning. "We need real meat."

"How long will it take me to do the line?" Vandaele asked.

"A week for the whole thing. In good weather, you spend two nights in the outcamps for every night here. You can do some of the pelting on the line, whatever's not frozen, but the more animals you take in, the slower you go. You might have to put in extra time here thawing out carcasses and pelting. If you take in too much, pull out some traps, shorten the line. The main thing is, don't get behind with the collecting. Anything dead in the traps gets chewed on pretty fast. At the same time, don't hurry. Do everything slowly and carefully. If it snows lots, expect to lose days. The more snow, the more work in packing the trail and uncovering and resetting the traps. A blizzard keeps you in. Don't even try to work through one. Can you smell a blizzard?"

"Any good wind could be bringing one in. The temperature goes up. The martens and rabbits and squirrels go crazy."

"That's it. And I've noticed that if there's a dull grey halo of cloud around a hazy orange sun, you can plan on snow. You've got maybe a day to dig in or get back to camp. What I do is just run up the line, collect any catch and hang the traps on trees. I prefer to sit a blizzard out at my main camp, working hides."

Dalziel took Vandaele back into the forest, off the river,

about a mile from camp. They came across a small swamp on a shelf near the base of the hill, surrounded by tamaracks.

"In deep snow, the moose bunch up here. Do you know what that means?"

"Yeah. Mother Nature's meat locker. We had one about a mile from our farm. It sounded like a railway yard sometimes. They seem to feel safer together, and once they've flattened the snow they can see the wolves coming at them."

"And there's plenty of those bastards around here. You'll catch a few in the traps and see more. Do me a favour and shoot them all, but don't skin them."

Vandaele laughed. "Too bad. They'd be nice to have in the tent."

"Sure as hell if you put them there, someone would drop in. A hundred-dollar fine knocks hell out of your profit."

57

A COUPLE OF weeks after their arrival, Vandaele and Dalziel built a raft and crossed the Nahanni, and a week later they were working at the extreme north end of the line. On the way there, they'd checked the gravel bars carefully for any sign of Eppler and Mulholland.

"That creek coming in over there drains Glacier Lake," said Dalziel.

Vandaele stared across the river. "No sign of any cuttings. Looks like it would be one hell of a thrash if we actually went up that creek."

"Yeah," said Dalziel.

They double-checked the gravel bars on the way back.

No sign of anything, but close to the main camp they were able to add to their larder. A breeze was coming up the river, blowing their scent away from a couple of caribou plodding up a bar, and they spent the next two days cleaning, cutting and carrying meat.

"That was good luck," said Dalziel as they bedded down after getting the last of the meat into the cache. "It's not fat meat, like moose, but it'll do for now. The dogs were getting hungry."

Dalziel settled into his sleeping bag to read for a while, placing a kerosene lamp on a log close to his head.

"Your back's been bothering you," he said, before opening the *Treasury*. "I could tell when we were moving that meat."

"A bit," said Vandaele.

"More than a bit.".

"I pulled it bad when I was in my teens, lugging stones for the foundation of our barn. It goes away."

Dalziel turned back to his book.

"Where'd you go to school, Dal?"

"In Vancouver. A private school."

"How come?"

"My dad was an engineer and inventor. He worked at home. He didn't like kids around because it broke his concentration, so we were all boarded at school through the week."

"How'd you get into trapping?"

"Boy Scouts. I think I read everything that Ernest Thompson Seton and Jack London ever wrote. Then one of the Scout leaders brought in a war buddy of his who worked on the telegraph line near Quesnel and trapped in his spare time. He took us up Lynn Canyon and showed us how to set snares and traps. I put my own line along False Creek. The headmaster saw me there one weekend and asked me why I wasn't at home. When I explained that I was trapping, he asked how much I made in a good week. I told him, and he said it was more than his salary."

"What did your parents think?"

"They had more important things to worry about."

"Did you finish school?"

"Yeah. Then I headed north with a school friend. We took the road to Smithers and followed the line to Telegraph Creek."

58

TWO WEEKS LATER, a light snow fell on the upper Nahanni area, and the temperature dropped from just below zero to minus 20.

"The fur on the marten we brought in is starting to look pretty good," said Dalziel one morning at their main camp. "Let's get serious and set traps. I'll head north and you go south."

A couple of days later, on his way back to camp, Dalziel was standing on the riverbank across from a small island separated from the shore by shallow water. He was watching the river, which now had ice about six inches thick extending six feet out into the stream. On the banks of the small island, on a stretch of mud just above the ice, he saw a familiar shape, a shape that shouldn't have been there.

It appeared to be a moccasin. The sun had melted the dusting of snow off it, so it stood out against the mud. It was lying directly above two sticks.

Dalziel tied Maverick to a tree, found a pole on the ground and placed it on the bank, pointing at the moccasin. Then he dropped his pack, slung his rifle over his shoulder and walked up to what looked like the shallowest water to cross, a spot where the ice extended clear across. The ice held. He walked down the island until he was lined up directly opposite the pole, went over to the edge and looked down.

The sticks were leg bones. They were still attached to a foot, and that foot was wearing a familiar moccasin.

"For God's sake."

So Wade must have tried to walk out the Nahanni on the ice, not going far before stepping into an overflow. His body got snagged on some rocks, probably, and torn apart in the current, the leg only recently released to wash ashore. There were no teeth marks on the bones, and Nazar's old moccasin was still intact.

Dalziel laid his rifle carefully on the ground. Gripping some willow in both hands, he lowered himself backwards over the bank. The mud was frozen enough to hold. He reached down with one arm and pulled at a leg bone. It broke loose. He reached farther and tugged at the moccasin itself, peeling it slowly off the mud. When he was sure the whole thing was free, he grabbed the bone by its top and lifted it, placing it on the bank. Gripping the willow again, he pulled himself up, shouldered his rifle and grabbed the bones. Holding them above the willow, he made his way back to the riverbank, where he rolled them up in his tarp, untied Maverick and headed for camp. There, he stored them in the Robin under some equipment, and went to make coffee and wait for Vandaele.

59

BY MID-NOVEMBER, THE thermometer was hitting minus 40 at night and two feet of snow covered the ground. Open water was a steaming narrow band down the centre of the river. Vandaele was learning how to scrape hides efficiently, and stretch and stitch them onto the thin boards that Dalziel had in his cache, most of them for marten but some larger ones for lynx.

"When you go after beaver in the spring, you stretch them flat, not folded over boards. Make willow hoops."

By November 22, the Nahanni was frozen solid. Dalziel announced that he would leave to check out Rabbitkettle Lake and the burned cabin at Glacier Lake. He attached the bonnet to the plane and put the heaters inside.

"I'll be back before dusk. While I'm gone, I want you to start on a new cache, a bit farther back in the bush and higher up than the old one. The trapping is going to be pretty good, and if you have any luck getting more meat, you'll need the space. Just copy the old cache, and use pieces of stovepipe to surface the uprights so the varmints can't get in. You'll have enough tin to reach a couple of feet down from the floor of the cache."

Vandaele nodded. He thought he should be accompanying Dal, considering the petition, but something in Dal's voice kept him from saying this. Anyway, Dal had waited so long that the ground was now covered by deep snow. There wouldn't be much of a search.

Dalziel didn't drop into either lake. Instead, he circled Rabbitkettle, gaining altitude over the spot where he'd dumped Wade's artillery, turning and still climbing along the south buttress of Mount Sidney Dobson, crossing high over the Rabbitkettle River, and then skimming down over small snowfields and glaciers, across the valley of Irvine Creek and over the hills to the Flat River. He came down just above the outlet of the Caribou River.

"Surprise, surprise," said Zenchuk, ambling out on the river ice to meet the plane.

"Good to see you, Nazar. I haven't got much time."

They covered the Robin's engine and set the kerosene heaters underneath. Dalziel retrieved the rolled-up tarp from the back of the plane, and they went into the cabin.

"A gift," said Dalziel in response to Zenchuk's questioning glance.

As Zenchuk poured coffee, he asked, "How'd you get the plane back?"

"Part of a long story."

"Let's have it. I need some talk. Last people I saw were Diamond and Newton, heading out from Faille's. They know that the cabin at Rabbitkettle is burnt to the ground, but it seems now that Amos Singletree and his family came out before we did last spring, from somewhere way up. He could've made those camps and for all Newton knows he could've blown up the cabin. Diamond was joking about it, but Newton's pretty frustrated."

"Well."

"So?"

"I flew meat into Yellowknife until the end of September and then got myself dropped into Simpson to see about the plane and meet up with Harry. The plane was still in stir, and no Harry. So I went over to Whittington's. Andy told me that he spotted Eppler in Vancouver."

"When it comes to a good story, Andy's as much to be trusted as a snake-oil salesman."

"He also heard, from Ernie Wainman, that one of Eppler's Newfies turned up in Telegraph Creek."

"And what does Andy make of all this?"

"He thinks Bill and Joe found gold. They had an argument. Bill killed Joe and took off for Australia with a bag of nuggets."

Zenchuk laughed. "No wonder nobody believes a damn thing Andy says."

"Some people do."

"The Turner brothers and the usual crowd at Andy's?"

Dalziel nodded. "Anyway, Andy and Stan Turner, with some prompting from Harry, drew up a petition that everyone in town signed, asking Truesdell to release the plane so that Harry and I could fly in on another search."

"Harry? I think I know what's coming. Tell me it's not so."

"It is so. I gave him a course in trapping, and he's working the line right now."

"A good joke. Truesdell will go crazy when he finds out. But I got the impression you wouldn't be putting Harry on that line. It's not safe, Dal. We might think Wade's finished or gone out of the area by now, but we can't be sure."

"Oh yeah?" Dal reached for the tarp, which he'd placed on the bed, and flipped it open.

Zenchuk stared at it for a long time. Finally he said, "So we *are* sure. We can stop watching our backs. But where'd you find it?"

"On the banks of a small island, just up the Nahanni from the mouth of the Rabbitkettle."

"He must've walked out on the river after you chased him away from the cabin. He must've gone into an overflow."

"Looks like it."

They resumed drinking their coffee.

"So now what?" said Zenchuk. "You'll probably get the plane back soon. Will you trap for the rest of the winter?"

"No. It's over, Nazar. Truesdell got his law passed—no more using your own plane to trap. Do you want to be a part of an outfitting business?"

"On that lake up the Redstone River?"

"Yeah. It's close to the action at Fort Norman and Eldorado. Mining and oil experts and investors are in and out all the time, and a lot of them want sheep. As soon as Truesdell releases the plane, I'll start flying in materials, and we'll build a fair-sized cabin."

"I'll work on the cabin in the summer, but I'm not interested in babysitting hunters. Can't stand most of them, like your admirer, Snyder. In October, you can fly me to Jackfish Lake or the Hyland River and I'll trap there. It's time this line was left a while."

"A deal," said Dalziel, and stood up. "If I stay any longer, the Robin'll be cold."

"Take that bloody thing with you."

Laughing, Dalziel wrapped the leg up again. As he flew toward Irvine Creek, he extracted it from the canvas and dropped it into the forest below.

"*In pace requiesat,*" he muttered, thinking as he said it that he meant it as much for himself as for Wade.

A half-hour later, just before dusk as promised, Dalziel landed at Vandaele's camp.

"What did you find?"

"Nothing new at Glacier Lake, but I dropped into Rabbit-kettle Lake too, across from the hotsprings. The cabin that was there is gone."

Vandaele shook his head. "Newton will never be able to figure out what happened up here."

"Something strange, for sure. Does it make you nervous about staying here?"

"No. There's nobody around. Anyway, I need the money. But I've been thinking, Dal. I can already see that the line's going to be too much for me. How about if you contact my brother Joe in Spruce View? They have a phone. If he doesn't want to trap, he'll know someone who does. It'll be $200 or so for MAS to fly someone in from Edmonton, but I'm sure it would pay. We'd get more pelts, and with a partner I could raft them all down the river."

"You could deck over the pontoons and come out on them. But if nobody turns up, you know what to do."

"Leave the pelts. Go down Irvine to Faille's. Don't worry, Dal. I've been stupid when it comes to prospecting, but I know enough about this river. The last thing I'd do is put out on it by myself on a raft."

60

I N   T H E   N E X T week, Dalziel and Vandaele walked the line, Dalziel south and Vandaele north, and then worked together at the pelting.

"Feel these marten pelts. The fur's thick and soft, and the skin's drying but still supple. This is ready to be taken off the board and folded. You have to do it at the right time."

Later, as they loaded a bundle into the cache, Dalziel said, "There's at least $500 here, Harry. Not a bad haul for a start."

"It feels good to be producing something for a change. I really appreciate this, Dal."

"We'll both benefit. I'm leaving in the morning. I'll trade these pelts and pay out the account at Jack's, take about $50 for gas and oil, and leave half of what's left in Daisy's cash box so you can get it on the way out."

The next morning, Vandaele followed the track and the fading sound of the Robin down the river until he stood where the ski tracks suddenly stopped. He'd never felt lonelier in his life. But Lisa and Maverick were there, rubbing against his legs. He was in a position now to make some real money, and he had *The Treasury of English Verse* all to himself.

6 1

"**D I D   Y O U   H E A R** about the cabin on Rabbitkettle?" asked Jack as he appraised and counted the pelts. "Newton and Diamond were through here at the end of September. Faille went up in the summer and found it blown apart."

Dalziel nodded. "I dropped in on Nazar a while ago, and he told me what Faille found, so I went to Rabbitkettle Lake. It's true."

"What the hell happened up there, do you think?"

"Your guess is as good as mine."

Flying down the Liard, Dalziel noted that the river trail was getting steady use: three dog teams mushing to Simpson, two heading the other way, and a half-dozen lone packers. The routines of winter were well under way.

He put down in Simpson and began attaching the plane's bonnet. Newton soon came clambering down the bluff toward him.

"Hello, Regis. Is there going to be good news for me at the wireless?"

"Transport radioed weeks ago and told us to release your plane."

"I'll be home for Christmas, then."

"You were gone a long time. I was worried."

"We did a proper search. I dropped in on Nazar, too, and he told me what you learned from Albert. So I went to Rabbitkettle Lake. What Albert told you is true. The cabin there is gone, blown up maybe."

"Where's Harry? I'll want to talk to him too."

"He decided to stay up there and trap."

"He's trapping your line below the Rabbitkettle hot-springs?"

Dalziel nodded.

"Dammit, Dal. He must've arranged all that before you flew him up there. You must've picked up supplies for him. Truesdell's going to see that he's been tricked and that you just spent two months training a new guy on the line. What are you going to tell him?"

"We were doing a thorough search. And since Harry was good enough to assist on the search, why not save him a long, hard canoe trip upriver to go trapping?"

"And how's he going to come out, since you won't be able to pick him up?"

"Either overland to Faille's, or on a raft. He wants me to send in an assistant on MAS. If that happens, he'll raft out. He knows the river."

Newton said nothing, just turned sharply and walked away. Dalziel, smiling, returned to fixing the Robin's bonnet.

He was betting that Truesdell would decline to come down to his tent and confront him, and he was correct. The next morning, after a good night's sleep, he was on his way to Yellowknife to find a passenger or a pile of freight bound for Edmonton.

"FO R G O D'S S A K E, Regis, leave it alone. I'm the one who should be upset. This fool trick of Dal's was aimed at me!"

"You're not upset because you got what you wanted. Dal's out of business. He's gone off to trap in the Yukon or run an outfitting business. But I've got to send Headquarters a report on an investigation that didn't solve anything."

"I never should have agreed to that patrol up to Faille's. It cost near $100 for gas, food and Diamond's guiding services and it resolved nothing. The story was clear before that— Eppler and Mulholland set out on the river in a skinboat and drowned. All I want you to do is confirm to everyone, especially the boys at Whittington's, that as far as the police are concerned the investigation is over. In fact, I'd like you to post your report just outside the door, so I don't have to talk to those idiots anymore, or the greenhorns who go in for a drink and come out believing that Bill and Joe made a gold strike up at Glacier Lake. Can you imagine what would happen here if the *Edmonton Journal* got wind of Whittington's and Turner's version of the story, and word got out that we were keeping the investigation open?"

"Shouldn't we be taking a closer look around Rabbitkettle Lake?"

"Even if I agreed to let you go there, which I won't, what would you find? Probably what Faille reported is correct. Dal confirmed it. But what does it add to the story? What's the connection?"

"That's what I'm trying to find out! Faille thinks Dal knows something he's not telling us, and I agree with him."

"Faille's another one who believes in the lost mine. His theory is that it's above the falls and he wants to prove it. Three years ago, he came down from there with a hundred pounds of iron pyrites in a sack. He dragged it into Whittington's and the boys started getting their outfits together for a rush up the Nahanni. Luckily, Clark was around and set them straight. Faille looked like an idiot, and he used his rocks to pave the path to his outhouse. The story about Bill and Joe finding gold up there vindicates him."

"Turner thinks Eppler could have killed Joe Mulholland."

"Eppler must've wished for years that he never told anyone that story about his murder charge. He never backs down from an argument, and he always says what he thinks, but he's a good man, and Jack and all the trappers who ever dealt at that trading post say that. Never had one single complaint about him. Turner, on the other hand, fights with everyone he deals with. So forget Turner. Forget Faille. Finish that report so Headquarters can release it to the papers, and post it outside my door so I can go back to my work."

63

AT NEW YEAR'S, the Dalziels got a sitter for Robin and danced the year out at the Strathcona Hotel on the outskirts of Edmonton.

"What a year," said Dalziel as he and June clung together, swaying across the floor with dozens of other couples.

"Count your blessings," said June. "You've got your plane. You've got trappers on the Coal River, Nazar's on the Flat, and Vandaele and that friend of his you sent in with MAS are on the Nahanni. You've put some stuff at Redstone Lake and started a cache. And that Frenchman we met at Snyder's has written about a hunt next fall."

"In a way, it was a good thing Truesdell forced my hand. I'll have the cache up in a month. We'll have the cabin and a dock built by midsummer, with Nazar helping. You'll be there by September, to take up camp cooking. Are you sure that outfitting is what you want?"

"It's what I want. I'm sick of you being up there and me down here."

Just after New Year's, Dalziel was loading building supplies for the cabin on Redstone Lake. The load was a light one, so he was hoping for a paying passenger for Yellowknife or Radium.

"Are you Dal?"

Dalziel pulled his head out of the loading door. Two young men, carrying rifles and large packs, and covered from head to toe in sheepskin, were looking at him questioningly.

"That's me."

"A mechanic at MAS sent us. He said you were making regular trips into the mountains west of the Mackenzie, and you might give us a deal on a ride to a place called Glacier Lake."

Dalziel nodded. He wasn't surprised. Just a few days ago the *Journal* had featured Peebles' full-page article "Land of the Vanishing Men," a result of his "northern odyssey," as Peebles himself modestly put it. Clearly, it was a bid for publication in the U.S. and the Pulitzer, and once again he had hit a public nerve.

Peebles' visit to Fort Simpson had evidently turned into a week-long bullshit session, with Peebles the main listener. Andy's version of the Mulholland-Eppler story, about which the RCMP were being mysteriously silent, was the centrepiece, and the only conclusion that any sane man could come to was that gold had been found by the two trappers somewhere around Glacier Lake or Rabbitkettle Lake. This discovery had resulted in a fight, as evidenced by the fact that two cabins had been destroyed, one possibly blown up, and Eppler had been sighted in Vancouver, no doubt on the run from the law. Andy's story was set against the saga of the headless McLeods and the subsequent searches for their mine. Faille, red-bearded mountain man, was quoted as saying, "I always knew it was above the falls."

And Faille, the Turners and some others from the Liard area were racing their dog teams in to get their claims staked before spring.

"Going to prospect, are you?"

"Did you see that article in the paper?"

"I did."

"We figure to stake the creek that flows into the lake from the south, not the big one coming from the west that everybody's staking. If our creek's full by the time we get there, we'll follow it up and over into the valley of the Rabbitkettle River and down to Rabbitkettle Lake."

"As it turns out, I'm leaving right away," said Dalziel. "I'm putting a hunting cabin up in the mountains west of Fort Norman. If anybody asks, you're working for me. My gas and other expenses will be $150."

"That's mighty generous," said one of the men. "MAS wants $200 *each*, and we have to wait until a plane comes back from Eldorado."

"I assume you have some equipment."

"In the terminal."

"Want to leave it and your packs in the plane overnight?"

"Good idea."

"Just stick your packs back there, and go get your equipment. Mind that window glass."

"When do we leave?"

"Break of day."

When he got home he checked his mail. There was a bill, a letter from his sisters at the nurses' residence in Vancouver, and a thin envelope that had his name and address printed carefully on it in pencil. The envelope had, he noted, no return address and was postmarked Vancouver. Curious, he sliced it open and found, on a scrap of lined paper, an unsigned, undated, hand-printed message: "Don't worry. I took care of your unfinished business up at the other lake. Be more careful next time."

He stuffed the envelope and letter into his pocket and sat a while, trying to catch his breath.

So Eppler had hunted Wade, bagged him on the river and made his way out. Eppler was alive, thank God. And Andy had seen him in Vancouver, on the way to Australia, most likely.

Dalziel thought a moment and then took the letter over to the coal-gas kitchen range. He snapped on a burner and held the letter in the flame, dropping the burning remnant on the top of the stove once the flare reached his fingers.

June came running into the kitchen. "What are you doing?"

"A letter of complaint," Dalziel said.

"I didn't realize you were so sensitive."

AFTERWORD

This story is an account of what did happen mixed with what *might* have happened. For what *did* happen—Bill Eppler and Joe Mulholland flying above the falls with Dalziel to trap one of his lines and the investigation of their disappearance—I have simplified complicated scenarios and dropped minor characters. But I stayed faithful to the main facts about my main characters—their names, what they looked like, how they acted, what they said and where they were at specific times.

What else could I do, my characters being real? In this I was like Shakespeare in his histories—an accurate analogy, I think, despite its ludicrous connotations. Shakespeare's real characters were and are better known than mine so my descriptions had to be longer.

There aren't many Nahanni buffs around as yet, and most of them are river rats—an odd bunch, stubbornly idealistic, not to say mildly deranged, like their hero Faille. Mainly, they are possessed by the river itself, and the area it drains, but also they ponder the books written by the area's pioneers: *The Dangerous River* by R. M. Patterson (also a river rat), *Nahanni* by Dick Turner and *Nahanni Revisited* by Al C. Lewis. Nahanni buffs have a website, whereon they take virtual tours of the river and Faille's cabin. They have an award-winning movie about Albert Faille, produced by the National Film Board. The more bookish and persistent among the river rats have gone from these sources into Nahanni National Park's Historical Resources Inventory, a package of taped and transcribed interviews with those who lived and worked in the area from the 1920s to the 1970s. These are the sources of Nahanni history.

Following, for those who have become intrigued by my characters and my story, are the biographies of my main characters, gleaned from the sources listed above and in order of their appearance in my book.

Bill Eppler was born in 1904 in Winnipeg. He stood trial for murder in the U.S. around 1920. He seems to have come to Fort Simpson around the mid- to late 1920s, probably with Jack Mulholland, with whom he'd teamed up in 1921 (according to Kraus). Clark, always careful in his statements, mentions him and Mulholland in 1929, "trapping up the Liard, right almost at the mouth of [later Clark says across from] Flett Creek." Daisy Mulholland, Clark says, came into the country later. This would probably have been in the early 1930s, when Eppler and Mulholland shifted their trapping to the area around Nahanni Butte. In July 1930, Eppler walked into Whittington's café in Fort Simpson and encountered two new arrivals to the area, Stan and Dick Turner. They asked him some questions about the Liard River, but according to Turner, Eppler didn't get a chance to say much as others were too busy talking. He did tell them that most trappers now used outboards on their scows and canoes—the Turners had paddled and lined their way to Fort Simpson. Eppler was involved in the pseudo gold rush in McLeod Creek in January 1934 and a follow-up trip the following May with Faille, Dick Turner and someone named "Old Ole." Eppler started the trading post with Jack Mulholland in 1935. Eppler ran their trapline by himself, and Jack ran the trading post with Daisy and Joe. Eppler and Joe were lost in the Nahanni area in 1936. The RCMP reports about this incident are hard on Eppler, who is sometimes "Espler" and sometimes trapping at Bennet Creek rather than Glacier Lake, sometimes in 1932 rather than 1936. Division File No. T 517-5 says "Mulholland was a greenhorn and Espler was reckless and foolhardy." It's hard to say where this information about Eppler came from; all of his trapping and prospecting colleagues referred to him with respect. Even Turner, who ran afoul of Eppler on the follow-up trip of May 1935, and who seems to have believed that he killed Joe Mulholland, spoke highly of him: "a man of good character, truthful, honest and intelligent (and an excellent bridge player), a gentleman and a true friend."

Albert Faille was born—"maybe in Bohemia"—in 1886, came to the U.S. at two years of age, lost his parents somehow and ended up in foster care in Pennsylvania. He ran off from there when he was eight years old and rode the freights. A hobo taught him how to trap. In World War I he joined the U.S. Army Corps of Engineers and went to France. When he got back he married Marion Carlson, and they had a child. Loving life in the bush, Faille drifted away from Marion into Canada, where he heard the McLeod story and headed for the Nahanni. On his first trip upriver, in July 1927, he met R. M. Patterson, who hitched his canoe to Faille's motor-powered scow. Faille taught Patterson how to line and track his canoe, and took him the final lap up to Virginia Falls. With Patterson's help, Faille built a cabin at the mouth of the Flat, but later found more lucrative territory up the Flat and built more cabins. These are visited by contemporary river trippers who light incense, offer up sacrificial paddles, mutter incantations and scrounge for souvenirs. Enshrined in rec rooms all over Canada are rusted tobacco tins, chewed-up moccasins and pieces of dried bark from Faille's cabins. In 1934, Faille spent the summer with Clark and Kraus sluicing for gold around McMillan Lake, testing the McLeod story. Faille quit trapping in 1943 to captain and maintain Truesdell's boat and serve as the doctor's handyman/mechanic. He needed a cabin in Fort Simpson then, so the doctor let him drag off the kitchen wing of his house. When Truesdell retired in 1950, Faille returned to his winter trapping and summer prospecting until sometime in the 1960s, when he retired as a trapper. He continued his summer prospecting trips above the falls. At about 85 years of age, he died in his outhouse sometime on New Year's Eve or Day 1973-74, and is buried in the Anglican cemetery at the centre of Fort Simpson.

Gus Kraus was born in Chicago in 1898 and came to the Nahanni area in 1934. Next to Faille, he was the grand old man of the Nahanni, a talkative, friendly, generous and imaginative person who seemed to take part in just about every event that happened on the Nahanni until his death in 1992. Gus's best move was to marry, in 1942, a Dene woman named Mary, née Denya, who could speak English, French and South Slavey fluently. For a time, the two resided and trapped at the hotsprings below First Canyon (now Kraus Hotsprings), spending their summers at Nahanni Butte. They made their living trapping (Mary, mainly), gardening (Gus) and, through the 1950s and 1960s, cooking (both of them) for oil-exploration crews. Gus also guided wildlife officials and police through the area. Former prime minister Pierre Trudeau, on his canoe trip from Rabbitkettle to Nahanni Butte, stopped to pay his respects to Gus and Mary Kraus at Kraus Hotsprings. Trudeau was followed by Jean Chrétien and Gordon Lightfoot. Mary and Gus retired to Little Doctor Lake, where Gus passed away at 94 years of age. There is a memorial to him at the lake. As of February 2007, Mary was still alive in Fort Simpson.

Harry Vandaele was born in 1908 in Spruce View, Alberta, to parents who had come from the U.S. in 1903 to homestead. In 1927, he went to Calgary and worked in a service station. He invested money in stocks and accumulated what his friend Al Lewis called "a small fortune," which he lost in the crash in 1929. In 1934, he and his fellow garage worker, Milt Campbell, heard about the McLeod Mine and decided to go for a look. They looked for two years and then gave up, turning to trapping. Vandaele engaged, with Dal, in what Lewis called "a conspiracy against the police," flying in on a search for evidence as to the fates of Eppler and Mulholland, a search that wasn't carried out. Instead, Dal trained Vandaele in trapping, and then flew out alone. Vandaele trapped through the winter of 1936-37, with the help of Lewis, who had been contacted by Dal. Dal's plane was "out of commission," so Lewis flew in with Mackenzie Air Services. The two friends rafted out on the Nahanni in June, losing most of their pelts and equipment in the process but becoming the only men known to have rafted out on the river at high water. In the late fall of 1938, Vandaele was forced to leave the north permanently because of back pain. He had a successful operation on his back, probably in 1942, at which time he was running his own mink ranch south of Calgary. In 1956, at the age of 48, he died of leukemia.

Milt Campbell seems to have left the Nahanni in 1937. According to Bill Clark, who kept in touch with him, he worked as the airport manager at Fort Simpson during the war, and ended up in the 1970s running a Texaco Station in Airdrie, north of Calgary.

George Campbell Ford Dalziel, known throughout the north as Dal, was born in Winnipeg and raised in North Vancouver, where he went to private school. He learned trapping in Boy Scouts and went north after graduating, ending up in Dease Lake, where he met Nazar Zenchuk. Dal and Zenchuk trapped and explored in the Yukon and NWT, ultimately attaching their own and other names to many geographical features: Zenchuk Creek, Sunblood Mountain, Hole-in-the-Wall Creek, etc. After a trek from the Liard River to the Mackenzie, Dal competed in a shooting contest with the famed pilot Wop May and won a trip to Edmonton, where he trained under Moss Burbidge as a pilot. He became Canada's flying trapper. After being legislated out of business by the Canadian government, he established a prosperous flying service in Watson Lake. Travellers on the Alaska Highway can see his log house there, directly across from the log hotel near the Alaska Highway signposts. During the war, Dal worked as a civilian pilot for the U.S. Army, training pilots and assisting in the construction of the Alaska Highway. In the late 1950s he sold his flying service and went into guiding and outfitting. He built another log house in Dease Lake as the base for his enterprise, which he called (unambiguously) Dalziel Hunting Ltd. He wrote on the fuselage of his plane, "Eat moose. Ten thousand wolves can't be wrong." He had exclusive hunting and guiding rights to the largest designated area in BC. Except for numerous run-ins with game officials, he conducted an operation that was praised by customers, none of whom died after being abandoned in the bush. In the early 1970s, Dal's youngest child and second daughter, Sherry, also a pilot, took over this business and Dal retired to Fulford Harbour, on Saltspring Island, BC. June died soon afterwards, and Dal did not respond well to this or to old age in general. As the judge who handled some family controversy over Dal's will put it, "He was not well; he was drinking too much; he was brooding because his pilot's licence had been revoked for health reasons; and he was getting old." He died, at 74 years of age, on December 26, 1982, and is still unmentioned in any official account of the Nahanni. Even the monument commemorating the bush pilots of Canada, placed in 1967 on Dome Rock in Yellowknife, omits Dalziel. Dalziel himself never talked much, and for obvious reasons was shy of publicity, which may explain his being forgotten. But he did, privately, document his activities. He carried a camera and kept a journal; the album and the journal are in Sherry's possession. In the journal, Dal describes taking Mulholland and Eppler to Glacier Lake, says that he advised them against occupying the cabin there and describes Eppler's jerry-rigged stove that started a fire the very first time the men tried to make tea. Of the subsequent investigation into the men's deaths, Dalziel writes, "Police believed I'd abandoned them."

Wallace A. M. Truesdell came to Fort Simpson in 1932 after service as Deputy Superintendent Duncan Campbell Scott's best field officer in the Department of Indian Affairs. Truesdell prospered in Fort Simpson for almost 20 years, gaining the confidence of most members of the community, though there were constant complaints. An early one, in July 1932, had the whole town, including Andy Whittington, Tiny Gifford and a host of officials (the agents for Northern Traders and the Hudson's Bay Company, the Anglican minister and Catholic priest, the soldier who ran the radio station and the RCMP officer), petitioning the authorities about Truesdell's sleeping habits: "The Doctor does not rise until about 3 p.m., and is generally available at the Hospital or his residence after 4 p.m. His hour for retiring is about 4 a.m." Later, Truesdell had a Model-T Ford shipped to the island, for which he had a road built so he could commute the quarter-mile from his house to Whittington's bar. He ran a farm and shipped vegetables to communities along the Mackenzie River; a type of soil in the area is named after him. Anyone responsible for mediating between whites and Indians in Canada's north is bound to be an object of controversy, but over the years, the people of Fort Simpson learned to appreciate Truesdell. Both Faille and Dick Turner became his fast friends. One thing that made Truesdell especially popular was that he presided over the birth of every child born in Fort Simpson. The island in the mouth of the Liard River is named after him.

Corporal Regis Newton came to Fort Simpson in the spring of 1936, with his pregnant wife. That summer he made a patrol with a special constable to continue the investigation of the Mulholland-Eppler disappearance. The only surviving result of this patrol is a map, dated December 30, 1936, of the country from the mouth of the Flat River up the Flat and Nahanni to Irvine Creek and Glacier Lake. It shows a route up Irvine Creek, over to Hole-in-the-Wall Creek, across the Rabbitkettle River a few miles above the hotsprings and up to Glacier Lake. The map indicates the campfire remains (thought to be Mulholland and Eppler's) at the mouth of the Flat, Faille's cabin on the Flat near Irvine, the remains of the burned cabin on Glacier Lake and a spot on the Nahanni above the mouth of the Rabbitkettle River "where traps, tarp etc was [*sic*] found on sandbar." One of Newton's sons thinks that his father and the special constable went right up the river, around the falls and to Glacier Lake, so maybe some of this map indicates the results of Newton's own investigations. Most assume that Newton never made it above the falls and all the information on the map was provided by Faille. Newton seems to have been in Fort Simpson for only two years. He died in 1971.

Nazar Zenchuk, after his experiences in the Nahanni area, went to Watson Lake with Dal and trapped in that area for many years. He married and had children, but his family life was erratic. So were his off-the-trapline habits. There's a persistent rumour that in the summer of 1948, Zenchuk arranged to meet a man named John Shebbach at the Caribou River camp. They probably intended to prospect—in 1938, the entire Nahanni watershed was closed to white trapping, and remained closed until 1953. In Patterson's version of the story, Shebbach walked in from Watson Lake. In Kraus's version, Dal flew him in. Months went by and finally someone inquired about him or (in Kraus's version) Dal mentioned him to the RCMP. Kraus guided the RCMP up to the mouth of the Caribou and found Shebbach dead, his body torn apart and scattered by animals. His journal was found—a record of 42 days of starvation. Right into his old age, Zenchuk seems to have enjoyed talking to others about gold up the Flat River, and offering to guide people into the area. He was a popular figure in the bars of Watson Lake—he was especially noticeable later in life because he had no fingers and held his beer glass between the palms of his hands. He introduced himself by asking people to stick a cigarette in his mouth and light it. He lost his fingers not on the trapline, but on the Alaska Highway, making his way home one night after the bar closed. He died in Whitehorse in a seniors' home.

Harry Snyder was born in 1882 in McArthur, Ohio. He sold casualty insurance in Kansas in the first decade of the 20th century, was a property developer in Texas and New Mexico (1911-15), sold life insurance (1916-19), then in 1920, in Chicago, started Snyder & Hay, a company specializing in corporate reorganization and income-tax problems. In 1932 he merged five failing oil companies in Montreal and incorporated and was chairman of the board of Champlain Oil, later a subsidiary of Imperial Oil. Pierre Trudeau's father was one of his vice-presidents. Between 1936 and 1939 he financed the expansion of the Eldorado radium mine on Great Bear Lake, but his arrangements collapsed with the start of World War II, and he was removed from the company's board of directors when it was discovered that he actually owned no Eldorado stock. He also started the first North American radium refinery at Port Hope, which provided uranium used to develop the atomic bomb. It seems that, due to his contribution to the war effort, he was given an honorary colonelcy in Canada's Black Watch Regiment. In 1937, Snyder led and funded an American-museum hunting expedition into Glacier Lake, despite warnings from various people that two trappers had recently died mysteriously in the vicinity. This was Snyder's third Canadian expedition—all were focused on collecting trophies for museum display. Snyder took time out from this expedition to host the Governor General, Lord Tweedsmuir, on his Arctic tour, meeting him on August 6, 1937, at Eldorado. Snyder flew Tweedsmuir to the Coppermine River and fed him steak during a picnic lunch in the Barrens. The tour lasted three days. Tweedsmuir was a popular novelist, publishing under the pseudonym John Buchan; Snyder's chatter may have inspired *Sick Heart River*, published in 1941, which describes a trip into a mysterious subarctic river that flows through a temperate valley and spreads a strange accidie or depression in men and animals. Snyder in fact suffered from some such illness, which he suspected he'd picked up in a hunt in Africa. There he wrote two books on hunting. *Snyder's Book of Big Game Hunting*, published in 1950, contains anecdotes of hunts in various parts of the world, including the Nahanni. In the book, a letter from Snyder to a young relative advises, "If you have any creative ambitions, whether as a tootler on the cornet or a business organizer, then take a minimum of six weeks every year hunting in the wilderness. You will return with your batteries recharged, and your views on men and opportunities in sharp focus." Sometime in this period, his wife Ida and daughter Dorothy disappear from his life, and a new wife, the nurse who came to Sundre to cure him, turns up. Though he was ill, he made a last trip into Glacier Lake in 1952. The ranch, and Snyder's vast trophy collection and library of documents about the Nahanni, burned to the ground in 1955, and Snyder moved to Calgary. Shortly after that he went to Tucson, Arizona, where he died in March 1972.

Bill Clark was born in Banffshire, Scotland, in 1901, studied engineering at Aberdeen University and came to Canada in 1923 to work for the Hudson's Bay Company at Port Simpson, north of Prince Rupert on the BC coast. He was shipped by mistake to Fort Simpson, where the company set him to book-keeping. When he was on a 1924 trip to Fort Wrigley to help out at the post there, his Indian guide told him the McLeod story and described the Nahanni River. He quit the HBC in 1929 and went up the Nahanni to prospect, ultimately, in 1933, focussing on McLeod Creek. In the winter of 1934-35, Kraus flew in to stake claims, and the two became partners; their explorations continued until 1939. Then Clark left the Nahanni to work on the Canol pipeline until 1945 and for Imperial Oil at Hay River until 1955. He prospected around Great Slave Lake and retired to the town of Enterprise, across the Liard River from Fort Simpson.